A PLACE AT THE TABLE

MEMORIES OF A LIFE WELL-FED

Essays by Carrie Seidman

Illustrations by Tracy Seidman

IBiS
BOOKS

1st edition 2023

ISBN-13: 978-1-956672-19-0 (Ebook edition)

ISBN-13: 978-1-956672-20-6 (Paperback edition)

Contents

Preface VI

1. Food and Fellowship 1

2. Pork, On the Hoof 6

3. Mangos 12

4. Waitressing 19

5. Brussels Sprouts 25

6. Cherries 32

7. Big Box Shopping 38

8. Chocolate 43

9. Bakery Dreams 49

10. The Lone Diner 54

11. Cookbooks 61

12. Gardening in the Desert 67

13. Favorite Foods 72

14. Pizza 79

15. The Skinny Critic 84

16. Foraging   89

17. Thanksgiving   94

18.. Lemonade   100

19. Family Dinners   104

20. Hunger   109

21. Mother Nature   114

22. Leftovers   120

23. Shrimping in Sarasota Bay   125

24. Playing with Your Food   131

25. Soup & Popcorn   136

26. S'mores   141

27. Holiday Cookies   146

28. Family Recipes   151

29. Christmas   156

30. Toots   162

31. Scents and Sense-ability   167

32. Strawberries   173

33. Food Consciousness   180

Acknowledgements   185

About the Author & Illustrator   186

For T.
With forever love and gratitude.

A Note on the Cover Art

This quilt square, by Tracy Seidman, is part of a quilt jointly created by the women of the Seidman/Berry family for their Grandma Berry's 90th birthday. It depicts the author and illustrator and their siblings and parents gathered around the Seidman dining table for a typical "family dinner" (for further elucidation, see page 104).

Preface

THIS COLLECTION GOT ITS start as a column called "A Place at the Table" which I wrote during the early 2000s for the late, lamented Albuquerque Tribune.

Enraptured at the time with the food writing of MFK Fisher, Ruth Reichl, and Laurie Colwin, I conceived of a non-traditional food column that would be more literary than academic, more human interest than instructional. My editors were skeptical, but the column eventually became popular enough that it was featured on the Scripps-Howard newswire.

That was back in the days when newspapers still had copy editors and the late Barbara Page, an award-winning headline writing and copy editor extraordinaire, loved the idea and became the column's greatest champion. I owe the success of many of these essays to her encouragement and literary finesse.

Though the Tribune's closure in 2008 spelled the end of the column and I moved on to other pursuits and geographical locations, over the years since I have been continually drawn back to the themes of food, family, foraging, and fellowship. Even within the wide parameters of my current position as an opinion writer for the Sarasota Herald-Tribune, I occasionally manage to slip in a column here and there that harkens back to those themes.

The original columns ran without recipes, but here I've matched each essay with a dish, mostly drawn from recipe cards written in my mother's perfect penmanship. Better still, each is accompanied by an original piece of art created just for this book by my very talented older sister, Tracy. My gratitude for her contribution goes far beyond the simple thank you note my mother taught me you must write if you're ever invited to someone's house for a meal. I have dreamed of this collaboration for a good part of my life.

So there you have it: a feast for the eyes, the mind, and — if you're willing to spend a little time in the kitchen — the stomach. I hope you enjoy reading about these memories as much as I enjoyed remembering and writing about them.

Bon appetite.

Carrie Seidman
Sarasota, Florida
September, 2023

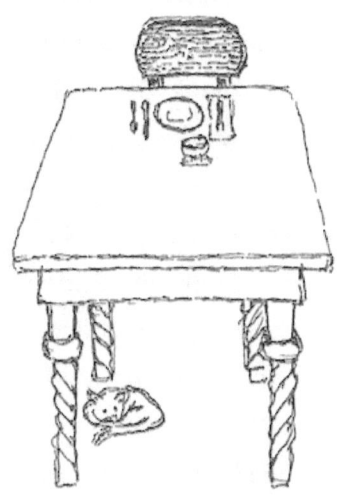

Food and Fellowship

ONE OF THOSE BIG reports with lots of confusing numbers in it crossed my desk recently. These are the kinds of things I rarely finish reading. As soon as I see percentages, parenthetical references, and phrases like "two-thirds of the 80 percent per person of restaurant meals," I start thinking about what I'm going to cook for dinner.

This was the annual survey of American eating trends and habits put out by the Institute of Food Technologists (food technologists?). And it was a little depressing because, basically, it said we are all going to hell in a handbasket as far as home-cooked meals are concerned.

According to these nutritional academicians, a dinner made "from scratch" is becoming as scarce as a street corner without a Starbucks. Over the last five years, the number of meals made at home has dropped another six percent, to less than a third of the population's dinner on any given night.

Now I can just imagine a lot of you rolling your eyes and saying, "Here she goes, off on some nostalgia trip about the perfect home-cooked family meals of her childhood."

Only that would not be quite accurate. While many meals of my younger years were home-cooked, they were far from perfect. And they almost never included my Dad, who worked in New York while we lived in Michigan, and thus commuted long distances and was rarely around. Even so, there were a lot of things I took away from them — and not just the critically important ability to blow milk bubbles out of my nose.

I learned meals were a time to dish the day's events, touch base with family members, and refine my debating skills. It wasn't as much about the actual dishes served as it was about the congregation.

That's not so surprising. Food and fellowship are inextricably linked in our culture. When you haven't seen someone for a while, do you call and say, "Haven't seen you in ages. Let's go grocery shopping." No, you say, "Let's have lunch."

Half of my pleasure as a restaurant critic came from choosing my dining companions. A good conversation can push a decent meal over the top or make a bad one digestible.

Even though he periodically goes through periods of intense mother-rejection, I still enjoy meals at home with my son. Not so much for the food, which, likely as not, is assembled late and capriciously, but for the new song he's composed and will likely hop up to play for me on the piano mid-meal or the news he shares from his workday, spent with more dogs than people.

I don't consider scarfing a sandwich in front of the computer or grabbing a bite solo a true meal. That's something else — an unconscious routine habit, obligatory fuel. For me, a real meal has to have two elements: food and company.

Which is why, despite all the disheartening news I read — like how French fries are the most popular food with kids under 6 — I found some encouragement in the report: "While the number of meals prepared at home continues to decline, Americans have a growing appetite for 'take home' restaurant food... People want to eat at home but not cook."

Even if we're not eating what we've made — the best of all worlds — at least we're eating together.

I also read about a survey of the dining habits of children of chefs; the idea was to find out if they are more adventurous eaters. What they actually found was the key to children enjoying a variety of foods was not necessarily the cuisine served, but the fact they regularly ate with family — and without TV.

As a single, working mother for most of my adult life, I know we're not likely to see again the world of slow-simmered pot roasts and home-baked breads for supper. Some nights it's bound to be pizza or Chinese takeout or grilled cheese and Campbell's tomato soup.

But instead of carving the roast, we can carve out time. Time to realize that food isn't the sole staff of life. Time to make a mouthful into a meal for the body and the soul.

No-Cook Chinese Chicken Salad

With a can opener and a store-bought rotisserie chicken, this can be put together in 10 minutes — for one or a crowd. Amount of ingredients depends on number you are serving; there's no need for precise proportions.

Ingredients

- *For the salad*

  ○ Romaine lettuce, chopped

  ○ Seedless cucumber, cut in half lengthwise and sliced into half moons

  ○ Green spring onions, chopped fine

  ○ Canned mandarin oranges

  ○ Rotisserie chicken breast, cubed or shredded *(or left-over cooked chicken)*

  ○ La Choy canned Chinese noodles

- *For the dressing*

  ○ Italian dressing

  ○ Teriyaki marinade *(I like Soy Vay brand Veri Veri Teryaki)*

○ Juice from oranges can

DIRECTIONS

1. Take out a large dinner plate for each diner and cover it with a generous layer of chopped lettuce.

2. Sprinkle cucumbers and onions over the lettuce, then arrange mandarin orange slices on top, followed by chicken.

3. Top with a handful of Chinese noodles and a sprinkle of onions.

4. Mix Italian dressing and marinade in 3/1 proportion, thin if desired with orange liquid and stir or shake vigorously. Serve in a pitcher alongside salads.

Pork, On the Hoof

HER NAME WAS LEWISSA, and she was a pig. Literally.

The baby pink porker arrived in a box equipped with breathing holes under the tree one Christmas morning when I was in junior high. The bouncing gift had a bright red bow and a tag that identified it as a present from my older sister to my father.

Now, my father was a man who liked big dogs, polo ponies, and Angus cattle (on a plate, very rare). He had never expressed the least bit of interest in pigs, and, in fact, wasn't even that fond of pork. (He preferred to gnaw on Flintstonian-sized steak bones and had a capped front tooth to prove it.)

But my sister, who'd moved away from home and was living in rural splendor in Connecticut, was insistent. In the middle of what she describes as her Earth Mother phase, she'd been appalled on a recent visit to see the amount of wasted food that went down the disposal at her family home. To her, the solution was simple. Get a pig.

After all, that was what she had done. Her own pet, lovingly named Bacon, gobbled the remnants of her gourmet cooking with relish. Simple. No waste, feed the critters, and — when the time comes — disappear the porcine presence to some pork-loving household.

But back to Lewissa. We kids came up with the name. My father went by L. William or Bill, shunning the first name he had long abhorred. So naturally, we found the feminized version the perfect choice for our new family member's moniker. Lewissa took up residence in the old dog pen next to the garage and happily scarfed up the apple cores, cheese rinds, and unpopular cereals that the four children kids still at home rejected.

Before we entered the house, a visit to her odoriferous pen was essential. Lewissa was always happy to see us, particularly if we needed to destroy evidence of not having eaten our lunch that day. We came to love her slobbery, hairy face, even after she became too big to qualify as adorable anymore.

Even my father was eventually won over. An early devotee of jogging, Dad would rise before the rest of the world was awake and run the mile to the end of the driveway to retrieve the daily newspaper. Soon after Lewissa's arrival, we began to hear curious rumors.

Did the Seidmans have a new dog, one uncharacteristically petite, and was that what they'd seen trotting along behind Bill the other morning? What kind of breed is it that looks so much like a pig, a neighbor wondered? And wasn't it quite amazing how those little legs could keep up!

The jogging couldn't counteract the table scraps, however. Eventually Lewissa got too big for the dog pen. My Dad's work took him more frequently out of town, and his fitness routine gave way to new challenges. Another one of the kids graduated and moved away, and the remaining ones' interests moved on to the next animal acquisition or boyfriend. The need for a breathing disposal waned.

Then one day, Lewissa disappeared.

In my family's time-honored tradition of pretending that uncomfortable occurrences had not, in fact, actually occurred, no one explained where our neglected pet had gone. But it didn't take a genius to figure out why the big freezer was suddenly so full of butcher-paper wrapped packages that bore labels like "chops" and "hock."

We were country kids. We'd seen our Shetland pony killed by lightning. We'd eaten steaks from the cattle on our farm down the road. But we also had our limits.

You killed Lewissa! we cried. *You killed our pet!* No way were we going to sanction the murder by cannibalizing her. (Note: This had nothing to do with religious dietary restrictions. Despite a Russian Jewish heritage, my father had rarely seen the inside of a synagogue. His children never had.)

And so the neatly wrapped packages remained, shoved to the side with a pang of regret whenever we were asked to retrieve something else from the freezer in the basement. One day, my mother's mother (a woman from staunch, puritanical New England stock who'd endured lean times during the Depression and believed waste was sinful) got wind of our rejection.

"Why, that's absurd!" she said. "I can't believe you would let a freezer full of meat go to waste!"

So, eventually, Gramma Berry ended up with a lifetime supply of pork. And the rest of us ended up with our memories of Lewissa, the pig who arrived in a gift box, went out in a freezer, and did some mean jogging in between.

Teriyaki Pork Shashlik

The easiest way to cut the meat for this dish is to freeze the pork and then let it thaw partially, so a sharp knife can easily slice it. Marinating overnight will increase the flavor and tenderness of the meat.

Ingredients

- Lean pork: butt, steaks or chops *(about ¼ pound per person)*

- Good quality teriyaki marinade *(¼ cup per serving)*

- Bamboo skewers soaked in water

Directions

1. With a very sharp knife, cut pork in thin slices and then into square cubes, so you end up with something slightly larger than a postage stamp and about ¼ inch thick.

2. Place pork into a container with a lid (plastic is fine) and cover it with sauce. Stir the sauce through the pork thoroughly, so every piece is well covered. Cover and place in refrigerator several hours, or preferably, overnight.

3. Thread pork slices onto bamboo skewers, making sure they touch but not compacting them. Place skewers on rack on top of cookie sheet.

4. Broil in the oven, approximately 10 minutes each side.

Alternately, these can be cooked on a charcoal or gas grill, also turning once.

5. Serve with/on rice or fried rice.

Mangos

I BOUGHT MY HOUSE for the tree in the front yard.

Well, OK, that isn't entirely true. But when I was wavering on making the biggest financial commitment of my life, learning from my realtor that the shoots coming off its long branches would, a few months hence, be dangling with mangos the size of an infant's head, pushed me over the edge. To a girl who grew up feasting on the apples and cherries of Michigan and who spent a decade foraging for wild huckleberries and raspberries in Montana, the idea of having my own tree, in my own yard, full of the tropical fruits I loved best was simply irresistible.

I never had a moment of buyer's remorse. Once late summer rolled around and my abundant crop grew ripe, my son and I enjoyed mango sorbet, mango salsa, and fresh mangoes with berries, over ice cream or (mostly) straight out of sticky hands. For dessert at one memorable dinner party, I thought myself incredibly clever to serve "Mango Three Ways" — fresh mango slices over mango sorbet with a dried mango embellishment.

Eventually I bought an industrial strength dehydrator, so I could peel, slice, and preserve those we didn't eat fresh. Its steady hum became my kitchen soundtrack for half the summer and its bounty became Christmas gifts highly anticipated by my five siblings and local friends.

Unfortunately, I quickly learned that my tree's alluring fruits — purple/red and oozing with milky juice at the stem as they came to maturity — were plenty irresistible to others, too. I'm not just talking about the egrets that neatly gnawed enough striations in the golden flesh to make the fruits frustratingly unusable. No, I'm talking about the steady stream of runners, dog walkers, bikers, and even drivers who passed by my unfenced yard, where the tree sits tantalizingly close to a public right of way.

Now, I believe most of my friends would say I'm a generous person. I donate to causes I believe in and charity cases that touch my heart; I've volunteered all my adult life, and I'm always stretched thin because I have a hard time saying no to anyone who asks for help. But when it comes to mangoes, I'm a regular Mrs. Scrooge. Do you remember the seagulls in *Finding Nemo*, whose screeching cries came across as "*Mine! Mine! Mine!*"? Guilty as charged.

When I (regularly) caught mango-pluckers standing in my yard, I did not react well. "But they were on the ground!" they'd say, as if all territorial rights were vacated once the fruit had dropped from the branch. One night when I was up way past my usual bedtime, I heard a vehicle idling out front and abruptly snapped on the porch light — to discover a small child halfway up the tree and his accompanying adults standing underneath with open shopping bags.

When I stormed out, they looked guilty and entitled at the same time. "We just love mangoes," they gushed. "I understand," I grumbled. "So do I."

One day I went to the gym before work, as is my habit, and realized I'd grabbed two shoes that didn't match. As I rounded the corner returning home, I saw an attractive young couple standing in my yard, each holding a perfectly ripe specimen. I had spent the previous weekend fending off July 4 pilferers, so my frustration was primed. I am not proud to disclose that I completely lost it.

"Maybe you could think about asking next time," I said sarcastically.

"But we were just wondering what they were!" said the man. "We've never seen these!"

Yeah, right. I told them to help themselves and stormed into the house. They sheepishly put the fruit on the grass and high-tailed it out of there — which ended up making me feel small and bad. But not as bad as when I got home that night and found a Starbucks gift card stuck in my door with an apologetic note from them.

You'd think that might have been enough to get me to lighten up. Instead, I plotted how to dissuade the plunderers less directly. A hidden camera? A sculpture of a large alligator? A lifelike robotic scarecrow?

A colleague at work, who felt similarly protective of her produce, said she'd posted "No trespassing! Violators will be prosecuted!" signs. I asked my son what he thought, and he gave me a look of exasperation and said, "You're just going to make people even madder, Mom."

The next year, a large and heavy package arrived from my older sister, a gifted artist with a clever wit. A note tucked in the box said, "Something you want and need." I figured it wasn't a handyman.

Inside, I found three beautiful hand-painted signs meant not only to improve the aesthetics of my scruffy yard but to send a firm, yet conciliatory message. One showed a delicate hand reaching toward a perfectly ripe mango, with an overlay of the standard black circle and cross slash that, even to a child, means, "Don't do it." The second had a giant camera lens and the words, "24-hour live streaming video at www.don'tpickmymangos.com." The third, with scattered illustrations of naked, dismembered or shriveled human figures, said: "WARNING: Mango thieves will be plucked, peeled, and dehydrated."

I attached the signs to some posts and planted them strategically in the yard, where they could readily be read from the street. Then I crossed my fingers and waited.

And you know what? It worked. Oh, people still stopped to gawk and point. But instead of venturing onto the grass, now they laughed, maybe snapped a picture or two of the signs, and walked on.

Let that be a lesson to you, I thought to myself. If you just approach a conflict with civility and good humor, people will respond in kind. So much better than uncomfortable confrontations or harbored resentments.

Sure enough, when I returned from the work the next day, all the mangoes were still there.

Now it was the signs that were gone.

MANGOS, THREE WAYS

It helps to have your own mango tree for this, but you can ask for (not steal) some from a neighbor or buy them at the store (in which case they won't be as sweet because they're never vine-ripened). You will need very ripe mangos for this recipe and you'll also need a home dehydrator for the third part of this recipe too, — an oven, even on the lowest setting, is too hot. They are not expensive and, if you have a constant source of fruit, they're great for drying everything from bananas to papayas to apples.

INGREDIENTS

- Mangos

- More mangos

- Even more mangos

DIRECTIONS

- *For the sorbet*

  ○ Peel very ripe mangos and put them and all the juices they release into a blender (an industrial strength one like a Vita-Mix is easiest, but any will do). If you use very ripe fruit, you should not need to add any sweetener or liquid whatsoever.

  ○ Pour pureed mango into a freezer/ice cube tray and put in freezer. Try to remember to stir it every half hour so it doesn't freeze into a solid cube. The higher the sugar content in the fruit, the softer it will remain.

- *For the fresh mango*

  - Peel mango and slice lengthwise, as you would a peach. Let it sit in its own juices, in the refrigerator. Again, with ripe fruit, you should not need any sweetener.

- *For the dried mango*

  - Peel mango and slice lengthwise, trying to keeping slices relatively uniform in thickness.

  - Arrange in dehydrator and turn on at medium-high heat. Depending on the moisture content of the fruit, within 24-36 hours it will have turned to fruit leather and you can peel it off the dehydrator tray.

  - Place in waterproof, plastic bags and store in refrigerator or freezer.

- *To serve*

  - Place a generous ball of mango sorbet (use an ice cream scoop) in dessert dish or stemmed glass.

  - Put a heaping spoonful of fresh fruit/juice slices over the sorbet.

  - Stick several of the dried mango slices on top, like a flag, as an embellishment. Serve immediately.

Waitressing

LIKE MILLIONS OF OTHER girls, when I was in high school, summer vacation meant a waitressing job.

It wasn't a glamorous or high-paying position — the wage at the time for someone who made tips being $2 and change — but it required no special training and was pretty much all that was available to someone under legal age.

Which is how I — at a painfully introverted and easily embarrassed 15 years of age — found myself marching around in a straw boater, hoisting a gigantic banana split in a silver bowl on an Egyptian-style litter, while clanging a bell and singing a testimonial to the diner who had ordered a "Pig's Trough."

You'll never know how fervently I prayed to the gods that summer that nobody I knew would ever set foot in that Farrell's Ice

Cream Parlour. All the free ice cream in the world couldn't make up for the humiliation of some studly upperclassman spotting me in my striped pinafore, splattered with chocolate syrup, or hearing my wobbly rendition of "Happy Birthday" sung to the back room kiddie party.

This was back in the pre-p.c. days when nobody had even thought about the unisex term "server." But even then, I realized waitressing was a thankless job of not only serving, but receiving... insults, mostly.

If you got an order wrong, it was your fault. If the cook burned the burger, it was still your fault. And if you did everything exactly right, but the customer had a fight with her mother that day and was beside herself with vengeful thoughts, it was still your fault.

A worrier and people pleaser, I wasn't cut out for this kind of work. It's humiliating to reveal that I am still, in my golden years, occasionally plagued by a recurrent nightmare in which orders are stacking up faster than my racing heartbeat and I can only move at the speed of sludge, with the staggered gait and impaired speech of a stroke victim. Wakes me up in a panic every time.

At 18, I graduated to working at an establishment that served liquor; in Michigan, that was the drinking age at the time. This was a step up only in terms of the 3-inch platform heels I had to wear as part of my mini-skirted uniform.

Plenty of the customers called me "babe," but I was one only in the sense of sheer naiveté. The first time a customer asked for "a Rusty Nail," I gave a responsive laugh, thinking he was making a joke. By the third time he asked — now with irritation — I reported him to the bartender... who informed me that a Rusty Nail was the name of a drink. Oh dear.

Whether it was because I was so gullible or so eager to please, I tolerated the inappropriate passes, the tipping stiffs on $100 tabs, and the abuse from inebriated parties. I learned to paste a frozen smile on my face when someone entertained their kid by allowing him to crumble cracker packets onto the floor or sent the bacon back twice because it wasn't crispy enough and then a third time because it was burned.

I started to hate food and everything that went with it. I'd go home after my shift, dump my syrup-splattered, grease stained, stinky uniform into the washing machine and stand under the hottest shower I could tolerate, hoping to burn off the layer of recriminations I'd received.

The day I had to stop someone who had hidden the entire table setting — including salt and pepper shakers — under her blouse, was the day I swore *Never Again*. Even if it meant working at a nursing home (the next summer) or going broke (the summer after that).

The perspective of years and many restaurant meals has only served to underscore for me that servers, like teachers, are among our most under-rewarded, under-respected, and over-abused members of the workforce.

And their greatest occupational hazard?

The likelihood that serving food will become so negatively tainted in their minds, they will never want to bring a meal they've prepared with love and pride to the table.

So the other day when my waitress (I mean server) greeted me with artificial cheeriness, delivered the wrong order, spilled coffee into my saucer, forgot to bring the check for eons and finally delivered it with a smiley face next to her name, I did the only thing I could.

I left her an enormous tip, in the hope it would help her toward a different career.

Farrell's Pig's Trough

Why anyone would want to make this, much less eat it, is beyond me, but it could be a big hit at a kid's birthday party. This is especially true if you can replicate the Farrell's presentation, which involved placing a huge silver bowl in the middle of a litter (stretcher) with horizontal handles and having a person on either end hoist it overhead and run back and forth while clanging an obnoxious bell and singing "Happy Birthday dear piggie..." Then I'd advise taking two Advil.

Ingredients

- At least three flavors of ice cream *(preferably more, though you needn't match Farrell's 28)*

- At least three ice cream syrups — chocolate, strawberry, caramel, marshmallow, whatever

- Bananas, slice lengthwise

- Chopped nuts, any kind

- Chocolate or rainbow jimmies *(sprinkles!)*

- Maraschino cherries

- Whipped cream

- Gummy bears, M&M's, or other small candy

DIRECTIONS

1. Take out large serving bowl and line it with the sliced bananas.

2. In the center heap at least two scoops of each kind of ice cream and a generous slosh of each of the syrups.

3. Sprinkle with nuts, jimmies, cherries, candies... anything with sugar will be a big hit.

4. Top with a generous crown of whipped cream. Serve center table with a big spoon for each child.

Brussels Sprouts

I WAS 25 YEARS old before I ever tasted a Brussels sprout. And discovered, much to my surprise, it was quite delicious.

Why surprise? Because I'd always assumed Brussels sprouts were vile and to be avoided at all costs. In fact, for many years, I never even knew they existed. Then, one day when I was about 10, I accompanied my mother to the grocery store and saw them in the produce department. I was at that stage when anything small — kittens, ponies, baby sisters to squeeze or to torture — held a special allure. And there they were, cute little buggers, looking like stunted heads of iceberg or a Lilliputian's cabbage.

"What're those?" I asked Mom, fingering the merchandise.

"Don't touch," she said. "Brussels sprouts."

"How come you never buy them?" She paused for a moment to consider her response, then let slip a rare glimpse of irrational bias.

"Because I don't like them," she sniffed. "I said don't touch!" Then she rushed me right on to frozen foods.

I thought they must really be dreadful if Mom wouldn't eat them because she cooked, and ate, just about everything. This aversion proved to be the one black spot on her nutritionally stellar record. (A quick Google search tells me Brussels sprouts promote a healthy immune system, colon, and skin, and protect against rheumatoid arthritis and birth defects; surely they would have fit Mom's "good for you" agenda.)

In other things culinary, Mom ignored boundaries, even when we wished she would. As kids, we were served exotic lettuces, beef tongue, and Indian curry sprinkled with raisins, coconut, and chopped peanuts while our Midwestern peers were enjoying tuna noodle casserole made with Campbell's cream of mushroom soup and topped with crushed potato chips. We had a huge garden in the summer, fresh herbs in a box on the windowsill, and friends who, after their first visit, made sure to ascertain what we were having before agreeing to stay for dinner.

Balance was important, too. You couldn't have rice and corn in the same meal because that was two starches. Nor broiled fish with parsnips — visually bland. And mashed potatoes and winter squash were too texturally synonymous to coexist. To Mom, these things mattered.

One of her favorite vegetables was succotash because it was such a tidy arrangement of colors, shapes, and "mouth feel" all in one nutritionally charged bundle. Which would have been just fine and good if it hadn't contained lima beans, which were my own produce nemesis.

I hated lima beans. I still do. They're the only vegetable I have to force myself to swallow. That is, if I ever ate them, which I don't. Most of the lima beans in my childhood went to the one family dog who would make them disappear, paving the way for me to have dessert. (Thank god for Bucks, even if the gastric distress rendered by my surreptitious snacks earned him the nickname of "Foo-euw.")

It wasn't until my son had become an official adult at 21 and was offered lima beans at a friend's house that I had the belated epiphany that I'd perpetuated just such a bias as my mother had.

"Lima beans? No thanks! They taste like chalk," he told the startled hostess whose home we'd been invited to for a fancy dinner. I was embarrassed, especially since I knew exactly where his rudeness had come from — I'd heard those same words coming out of my own mouth.

Afterward I asked him if he'd ever tried lima beans. He admitted he hadn't.

"But that's what YOU always said," he complained, looking wounded at the attack.

For a long time, I felt pretty bad about this. Like Mom, I'd always prided myself on my open-mindedness about food and I thought I'd transferred that well to my son. When he was little, I remember envious friends begging me to tell the secret of getting him to eat, and even request, salads and vegetables. On a trip he took to China with his martial arts group during high school, he ate animal innards I never would have touched. These days he's disappointed when a sushi restaurant doesn't have seaweed salad and delighted when a menu features something he's never tried before.

But never had a single lima bean crossed his lips, and the only one to blame for that was me.

Our tendency is to become less adventurous in our eating as we grow older. The foods we introduce to our children early on can shape their later eating habits more than we may ever know.

So when I was asked recently to read Dr. Seuss's "Green Eggs and Ham" to a class of third graders during a county-wide day of celebrating the cherished author's works, I asked the teacher if I could introduce an "activity" as well. From past experience, I knew I'd get a better reception if that activity was out of the ordinary.

On my way to the school, I stopped at the Whole Foods Market, grabbed a takeout container and cruised the salad bar, choosing the most unusual, un-childlike items I could find: pickled okra, Greek olives, tiny whole baby corn, hearts of palm, curried chick peas. (This only set me back about a week's salary.) Then I arranged everything invitingly on a big tray.

After we read the book and talked about how important it was to give a new food a chance before rejecting it, I invited each child to come up and choose to try something they'd never tasted before. Most of them eyed the selection ominously, searching hard for something familiar. The most identifiable item (the corn) was the first to go. As for that okra? Well, I'll just say it's a good thing I like pickled okra.

One little boy, however, defied the odds and made a game of showing his classmates his bravery in eating the exotic. He sampled everything and asked if I had any more marinated mushrooms when they ran out.

When I commended him for his adventurousness, he said there was nothing there his parents hadn't already introduced him to; they were chefs, he said, and he'd grown up in their restaurant kitchen.

No wonder, I thought.

After a moment, I thought to add, "And is there anything you don't like to eat?"

"Yeah," he grinned. "Green eggs and ham."

Roasted Brussels Sprouts with Dried Cranberries

I'm not the only one who has discovered the joys of Brussels sprouts; the roasted version is a popular item on many a trendy restaurant's menu today. This recipe comes from a friend who brought it to my annual communal Thanksgiving open house for readers. They were so popular they disappeared before I got any, so I got the recipe from her and have made them many times since just for myself.

Ingredients

- 1 pound fresh Brussels sprouts, trimmed and halved

- Olive oil

- ½ cup dried cranberries

- ¼ cup champagne vinegar *(I've also used leftover champagne, if that's something you have around)*

- 1/4 cup honey

- Salt and pepper to taste

Directions

1. Preheat oven to 375 degrees F.

2. In a large bowl, toss Brussels sprouts with olive oil, and season with salt and pepper.

3. Spread sprouts on a baking sheet and roast for 20-25 minutes until tender and lightly browned.

4. While the sprouts are roasting, make the sauce. In a small saucepan over medium heat, whisk together champagne vinegar and honey until honey is dissolved.

5. Bring the mixture to a simmer and cook 5-7 minutes until thickened, adding a tablespoon or two of water if necessary for best consistency.

6. Remove from heat and stir in dried cranberries. Drizzle sauce over roasted sprouts, gently toss, and serve.

Cherries

A NUMBER OF YEARS ago I went back to Michigan — land of sweet cherries, corn on the cob, and my birth — for a family reunion. Since none of my family actually still lives there, it had been a long time since I'd visited. But after passing waving fields of cornstalks and highway signs for cherry pie, it reminded me of how certain places and periods of your life are inextricably linked to certain foods.

Take those sweet cherries, for instance. To me, cherries meant summer camp. In mid-June or early July, my mother would pop one of her euphemistic "pep pills" (I later found out these were amphetamines), stick her daughters in the station wagon, and embark on the three or four-hour drive north to drop us off at Camp

Arbutus, a summer haven for girls tucked alongside a sparkling lake deep in the northern pines.

The travel route passed through prime cherry-growing territory, and the seasonal timing was perfect. The roadside was dotted with ramshackle stands sporting crudely lettered signs urging: "Fresh sweet cherries!" "Life's a bowl of cherries!" "You can never have too many!"

Well, that last one was wrong, anyway.

We managed to prove that just about every trip by downing so many of the juicy, purple globes that pit stops were as frequent as pits. On the day I didn't quite make it to the next one, my ever-peppy mother tied a sweater around my waist and claimed no one would notice. But she forgot about my sisters, who evilly snickered and held their noses for the rest of the trip. The incident still makes me feel traumatized.

Then there was camp food itself. This was back in the days before convenience, prepackaging, penny-pinching, or reliance on frozen institutional foods. At Camp Arbutus, a plump and jovial woman we knew only as Cookie regularly turned out heaping platters of gooey sweet rolls, fist-sized meatballs, and fresh succotash that pretty much guaranteed you were going to go home a few pounds heavier. Occasionally, the campers heralded her in chorus:

Cookie, Cookie, listen while we sing to you,
Cookie, Cookie, you're a part of camp life too,
Anyone can make a bed, anyone can sweep,
But it takes a Cookie, to make us things to eat!

After hours, we'd pick the lock on the camp kitchen pantry and steal loaves of squishy Wonder bread — the kind my Mom referred to as "flannel bread" and refused to buy — and bring it back to our cabins (strictly prohibited, of course) to make finger-kneaded "bread balls." They were just as gross as they sound.

It's amazing, really, the things you think taste good at that age.

The last summer I spent at camp — before I rebelled and instead worked as a waitress at a Farrell's ice cream parlor, running up and down the aisles clanging a bell when someone ate a whole "Pig's Trough" — I acquired a taste for coffee.

My junior high heartthrob had broken up with me by *Dear Carrie* letter, and on a field trip to nearby Traverse City I spent a whole afternoon reading Kahlil Gibran and dropping tears and spoonfuls of coffee over a bowl of vanilla ice cream and apple pie in an old-fashioned diner. The items remain inextricably entwined in my mind still — the bitter coffee, the sweet cream, and the poetry I then found so poignant and profound.

I don't get back to Michigan much anymore. There's no family or home left there and, other than memories of summers at the "big lake," it doesn't hold much allure. One of the last times my entire family was together there was the occasion of my parents' 60th wedding anniversary decades ago.

We rented a cottage in "Skunk Hollow," just down the road from the one we'd spent summers in as kids; the one that eventually succumbed to the rising waters and cascaded in a heap of splinters into the lake. (I always thought that was kind of a fitting end; I wouldn't have wanted some other family to live there.)

While there, my siblings and I indulged in all the old favorites: the moist-tender corn on the cob, cooked for barely a minute, rolled in sweet butter and sprinkled with salt and pepper; maple-walnut fudge, wrapped in white paper at a tiny shop and devoured in tiny slivers sliced off with a plastic knife; fat cantaloupes sliced in half, emptied of seeds and scooped out by the spoonful like you were eating the dish itself.

Not much had changed. The roadside stands were still there, the waving cornstalks stretched as far as the eye could see. White fish, a native of the Great Lakes that has nothing in common with the garbage fish that also goes by that name, still ranked high on every restaurant menu.

And cherries. So many cherries that... well, let's just say no pep pills were necessary to get us trotting.

Fresh Cherry Cobbler

The cherries we ate from the farm stands in Michigan were deep purple sweet cherries. (If you buy too many, these are also a great kid treat frozen.) For the best cobbler or pies, use pitted red, sour cherries.

Ingredients

- ½ cup butter

- 1 cup flour

- 1 ¾ cup white sugar, divided

- 1 tsp. baking powder

- 1 cup milk or buttermilk

- 2 cups pitted sour cherries

- 1 Tbsp. all-purpose flour

Directions

1. Preheat oven to 350 degrees. Place butter in a 9x13-inch baking dish and put in the oven to melt while it is pre-heating. Remove as soon as butter has melted, about five minutes, and spread to cover bottom of dish.

2. Stir together 1 cup flour, 1 cup sugar and baking powder. Mix in milk or buttermilk until well-blended, then pour the batter over the melted butter. Do not stir.

3. Place cherries in a bowl and toss with remaining ¾ cup sugar and additional Tbsp. flour. Distribute cherry mixture evenly over the batter in the pan. Do not stir.

4. Bake in the preheated oven until golden brown, about 50-60 minutes. Remove and let sit for 10-15 minutes. Serve warm, embellished with whipped cream, sour cream or clotted cream.

Big Box Shopping

I WENT TO COSTCO the other day.

It's something I don't do much anymore since my household at the moment consists of one light eater and a cat who often prefers to import her meals from the backyard. (And I do wish she'd finish the tails.)

With my son now on his own, my parents gone, and my beloved dog a distant memory, there's not much need for a twin-pack of gallon milk jugs, a two-pound wedge of brie, or a Santa-sized sack of kibble.

But, I swear, there has to be something in that fluorescent, warehouse lighting that creates the unshakable conviction that you simply must have that five-pound bag of sugar snap peas and that those two dozen kiwis can't possibly all ripen at the same moment.

I can never resist. I simply must have those elegant peppers in reds, yellows, and purples, even if there are enough to make ratatouille for the entire city. Mmmmmm, mangoes, perfectly ripe. Surely I can eat a dozen without dire consequences? And how can I pass up that pound block of yeast when it costs barely more than the grocery store charges for the little envelopes holding less than an ounce?

I remember the first time I ever set foot in one of these citadels to American gigantism and overconsumption. It was shortly after I'd moved to New Mexico following my divorce to live on my family's remote ranch in the northeastern part of the state and contemplate my unanticipated future.

One morning my sister, who'd already spent two decades there, started loading empty coolers (plural) into the back of her pickup in preparation for our three-hour drive to Albuquerque.

"For the groceries," she said matter-of-factly.

I'd never lived more than five miles from a supermarket before. Coolers were for picnics and keeping beer cold on a hot summer day, not for keeping lettuce from wilting on a 175-mile summer drive home from "town." Ice cream? That was out of the question, unless you had a source for dry ice.

"I must have something to learn about grocery shopping in the West," I thought. I was game. With the closest grocery store 45 miles away, it made sense to lay in supplies for unanticipated obsessions.

But I wasn't quite prepared for the magnitude of this new kind of store or its mega-size offerings. As my sister tootled merrily up and down aisles stacked with goods, floor to ceiling, tossing things onto her flatbed with wild abandon, I staggered around with a glazed look trying to imagine just what one did with a pound of dried parsley flakes or 4 liters of olive oil.

As I recall, I did buy a few things. A six-pack of canned black olives that I figured couldn't go bad. A 5-pound sack of baby carrots. (I like carrots.) Those I could justify, although what possessed me to think I needed that enormous plastic sack of heat-and-serve Italian breadsticks, I'll never know.

I now live in a town large and metropolitan enough that 24-hour gratification is possible, so I can no longer find as much justification for super-sizing purchases. But I still go to Costco once in a while, with every frugal intention. And I inevitably come home with too much of too many things. Why?

It's not cheaper, at least not when you factor in what I throw out because it's gone bad before I've gotten to it. The quality isn't always better either, although the oversized produce is lovely. And I haven't found those olives I love so much anywhere else.

It's certainly not because I have heeded the dire warnings of the Homeland Security Department to stockpile my bunker.

I've never been so poor that I've gone hungry. I've never had to wonder where my next meal was coming from. And yet a full larder gives a sense of security beyond the mere reassurance of knowing you are not going to starve to death.

There's a lovely feeling of abundance in opening the refrigerator door to see something other than that tired old box of baking soda and the ascetic container of yogurt.

It's the steadying feeling of the pioneer woman when hubby's elk was hanging in the lean-to, the root cellar was full of squash and corn, and she'd already been to the creek for that day's water.

Simply, it says this: I am well provided for. Life will go on.

GREEN CHILE CHICKEN ENCHILADAS FOR A CROWD

You can make this recipe as easy or as difficult as you like, using a store-bought rotisserie chicken and canned gravy for the former, or roasting your own chicken and making gravy from scratch for the latter. (If you're more ambitious than I am, you can even make the tortillas from scratch.) Do try to get New Mexico Hatch green chile for the best flavor; if you don't live in the Southwest, you may have to order it online. Make enough for leftovers; enchiladas always taste best on the day after you make them.

INGREDIENTS

- Two dozen white corn tortillas

- 4 cups shredded or chopped cooked chicken, light or dark meat

- 1 cup Hatch green chile, chopped

- 4 cups chicken gravy, scratch or homemade. *(You can even use diluted cream of chicken soup in a pinch)*

- 2 cups shredded cheese — a Mexican blend is best, but any will do

DIRECTIONS

1. If you make your own gravy (use a roux and half chicken broth/half milk) do that first. Add the green chile.

2. Grease a 9 x 13-inch pan. Spread a thin layer of gravy on bottom of pan.

3. Place ⅓ of the tortillas slightly over-lapping, in single layer on bottom of pan. Sprinkle half chicken over tortillas, sprinkle with ¼ of cheese and ⅓ gravy over all. Repeat the layering with another ⅓ of the tortillas, the remaining chicken, another ¼ of the cheese, and another ⅓ of the gravy. Finish with a final layer of tortillas topped with remaining gravy, which should fully cover each tortillas. Sprinkle the remaining half of the cheese over all and cover dish tightly with foil.

4. Bake in 350-degree oven for 45 minutes covered and 15 minutes more with foil removed. Let sit for 10-15 minutes before serving.

Chocolate

I DON'T LIKE CHOCOLATE.

There, I've said it, though something tells me it should have been more momentous. Delivered in a dark confessional with the appropriate amount of remorse and requirement of Hail Marys. Or at a 12-step meeting, in a quiet, somber tone:

"My name is Carrie, and I do not like chocolate."

Because right on the face of it, if you admit you do not care for the substance that soothes women with PMS, cranky children, and minor relationship tiffs, you are immediately suspect to 99 percent of the population. Women especially, since chocolate is their palliative of choice.

"That is just wrong," a new girlfriend who'd yet to learn of my failing said the other day, after I declined to sample some double fudge ripple chocolate ice cream with chocolate truffle nuggets. "Did your parents drop you on your head when you were a baby or what?"

"Well, I do like white chocolate," I protested feebly.

She gave me a withering look that made it clear she was debating whether this friendship was worth pursuing at all.

"Don't be ridiculous," she scoffed. "That's not even remotely the same thing."

Not liking chocolate, of course, is not on a par with not liking, say, arugula or caviar. Those can be acquired tastes, sometimes not acquired until well into adulthood — or ever — but you'd find plenty of company for your aversion. It is more on the level of admitting you pick your nose in the car or lie regularly to your lover. A disgusting trait at best, a heinous character flaw at worst.

How I came to refuse the rich, mellow caress of a Hershey's kiss or the bittersweet bite of a dark truffle, I don't know. It's been that way as long as I can remember. When my siblings were battling over M&M's and candy bars, I was opting for Dots, butterscotch Lifesavers, and red licorice. (Don't even get me started on chocolate licorice which, as my friend would say, is not even remotely the same thing.)

Sometimes I lie and say I'm allergic in order to elicit sympathy instead of scorn.

"Oh my god, you poor thing," is the usual reaction. "What happens if you eat it?"

"Mmmm... hives," I murmur dismissively.

"Is that all?" is the incensed retort, as the estimation of my moral fiber plummets.

More than once, my distaste has put me in a precarious social position. I particularly remember an elegant dinner my husband and I attended at a wealthy client's home during the brief time I was married. After a multicourse gourmet dinner, the hostess produced her "specialty" for dessert — a rich and heavy chocolate gateau embedded with a plethora of nuts.

My husband disliked nuts as much as I dislike chocolate. He gave me a pointed glance.

"You eat it," he whispered.

"No, you," I hissed.

I pleaded preservation of my figure and settled for a slender slice. He covered his tiny mountain of rejected nuts with his napkin. Maybe it wasn't the reason, but we were never asked to dinner there again.

When I had one of those big zero birthdays, I celebrated with a trip to California with several girlfriends. At the culmination of the birthday dinner at a gourmet restaurant — and, by the way, if you heard anything about someone doing the splits on the bar wearing a foot-tall pink tiara reading "Birthday Queen," it wasn't me — the waiter brought a mound of warm fudgy pudding cake topped with a rich, melting blob of chocolate ice cream and a single candle.

I made a wish. Well, two actually. The first I kept to myself. The second was a fervent hope that my declining a bite would not cause derision. This wish was immediately denied.

"Seriously?" said Christine.

"You know, we love you, but you are very weird," Annie added.

Then she and the others reached over with their spoons.

"Maybe it's not so bad that you don't like chocolate," Luanne said, licking her spoon, dazed and blissful. "Can I have that last bite?"

Whether in food, fantasy, or religion, tolerance is a good thing, I told them. Maybe you don't care for mushrooms. Or eat red meat. Or perhaps you draw the line at raw oysters and escargot.

They weren't buying it, but they humored me. After all, it was my birthday. And they had to admit that whatever you turn down leaves more for someone who adores what you abhor. That's my story, anyway, and I'm sticking to it... one day at a time.

"My name is Carrie. And I don't like chocolate."

SAUCEPAN BROWNIES

This recipe has been in the Seidman family for ages. Needless to say, I don't eat these, but I've given them away as gifts many times and added them to the Christmas cookie plates we share with friends after someone complained that none of the cookies contained chocolate. If you want to add to the decadence, top them with a simple confectioner's sugar/cocoa/butter frosting after they've cooled.

INGREDIENTS

- 1 cup butter

- 6 Tbsp. good quality cocoa

- 2 cups sugar

- 4 eggs

- 2 tsp. vanilla

- 1 ½ cups white flour

- 1 cup chopped nuts *(optional)*

DIRECTIONS

1. Preheat oven to 325 degrees. Grease and flour 9 x 13-inch pan. Melt butter in a medium saucepan. Remove from hit and stir in cocoa and sugar. Mix thoroughly. Add eggs, mixing them in thoroughly, and then vanilla.

2. Mix in flour in two portions, making sure it is fully incorporated. Add nuts (unless your husband doesn't like them) and pour mixture into prepared pan, making sure it reaches to each corner.

3. Cook in preheated oven for 30-45 minutes; do not overbake. Edges should be firm and middle springy.

4. If you choose to frost, wait until the brownies have fully cooled.

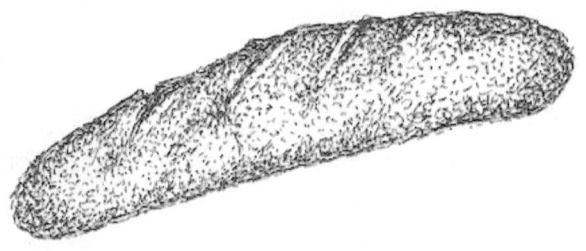

Bakery Dreams

EVERYBODY HAS A WALTER Mitty dream, and mine has always been to go to pastry school.

So when I saw Aude Laau at Le Paris French Bakery one day, I asked if I could come bake with her some morning. She rolled her eyes in a way that said both, "What would you want to do that for?" and "You have no clue," and then agreed.

"Come at 10," she advised, in her strong accent. "And don't wear black."

Of course by 10, Aude Laau (whose name is pronounced "owed louw") has already been at the bakery for hours, her 18-month-old daughter, Naomi, napping in a playpen in the corner of the kitchen. Even though she has relinquished the bread baking to an overnight crew, she still puts in a "mee-nee-mum" 12-hour day, seven days a week; during holidays, more like 18.

Laau, who is 33, has a thin face and baby-fine brown hair gathered into a bunched-up ponytail. She wears faded black jeans that hug a figure of barely 100 pounds and are constantly dusted with a fine sheen of flour.

"I only eat bread and butter all day here," she says, commenting on her size. "But I am never sitting down."

At first she looks too slight to be capable of a baker's manipulations. Then you see her hands are large and strong, with big knuckles and a rough redness.

"Turnovers," she says brusquely, hefting a slab of chilled dough from the cooler and slamming it down on the metal work surface. "First, through the *lamineaux*."

She feeds the dough through the "spreader," pulling and pushing as it slides through to make an even rectangle.

"You try," she says, looking encouraging and stern at once.

The dough overlaps in one section and tears in another. She smiles knowingly. Without comment, she pushes with a single finger, hammers slightly with the base of her palm, and makes the hole disappear. She continues stretching the dough, cuts it with a tiny sharp instrument — "You see this? Thirty dollars from France" — and then plops down uniform globs of cherry filling at regular intervals.

"Too much!" she says, swiping a teaspoon across one of my own uneven piles. "And you forgot to cut the edge first."

She does what I do in less than a quarter of the time. Her hands fly across the top of a King Cake, making an intricate pattern of fine slashes.

"Too deep," she says of my own attempt. Then she smiles forgivingly and adds: "It's OK."

I'm stunned that my hands, once quite capable, now seem thick-thumbed and uncoordinated. As I painstakingly work to mold four erratic turnovers, she creates a perfect row of a dozen while at the same time tending to a cranky Naomi, answering the phone, tossing a handful of flour into a nearby kneading machine, giving orders to an assistant, and delivering opinions in a rapid-fire stream.

"I guess I am sort of perfectionist," she admits, in her heavy accent. "After all, this is family bakery, not Albertsons. I want the customer to be happy." But she wishes her customers knew that:

"An eclair is not so huge. It is like a little finger."

"Petit fours is not just little cakes. It is any little sweet thing."

"True French bread is water, flour, salt, yeast. Nothing else."

Other things she prefers remain secret: "For the pastries, it is about one part butter to two parts flour... no, more like" (here she draws a 3/5 in the dusting of flour on the counter, then holds a finger up to her lips) "but, shhhh ... don't tell."

By noon, she takes a quick break to pick up her two older sons from school. As she dashes out, I ask if she enjoys her long days. "I guess I must love it because I am doing it, *non*?" she says. Then she turns the table. "And you like being a writer?" I nod. "That's good," she says, kissing me on both cheeks.

And politely refrains from adding: "Because you'll never make a pastry chef."

French Bread

If you want these make these as baguettes, you can buy special round-bottom loaf pans to get the traditional shape and crust. A pan of hot water placed on the bottom of the oven while baking can also lead to a chewier crust. Remember that these loaves contain no preservatives, so they are best consumed within a day, or two at most.

Ingredients

- 6 cups unbleached white flour

- 2 generous Tbsp. active dry yeast.

- 1 ½ teaspoons Kosher salt

- 2 cups warm water *(warm, but not hot, to the touch)*

- 1 Tbsp. cornmeal

- Optional: 1 egg white mixed with 1 Tbsp. water

Directions

1. Grease large baking sheet and sprinkle with cornmeal. Set aside.

2. Dissolve yeast and salt in ½ cup water. Once dissolved, add the remaining water and 2 cups of the floor and blend well. Continue adding remaining flour gradually until fully incorporated.

3. Knead dough on a lightly floured surface, adding more flour if necessary to prevent sticking, until smooth and elastic, approximately 10 minutes. Shape into a ball, place in a bowl greased with oil or no-stick cooking spray and turn over once. Cover with a clean dishcloth and let rise in a warm place until doubled in size, about one hour.

4. Punch dough down and divide in half. Turn out halves onto a lightly floured surface, cover with cloth and let rest for 10 minutes.

5. Roll each half into large rectangle, then roll up tightly, starting from a long side. Taper ends and moisten edge with water to seal.

6. Preheat oven to 375 degrees.

7. Place loaves seam-side down on cornmeal-dusted baking sheet. Brush each loaf with egg white/water, using a pastry brush, then cover with a damp cloth and let rise until nearly doubled, about 30 minutes.

8. Lightly slash tops of loaves on diagonal, 3 or 4 cuts per loaf, about ¼ inch deep. Bake in preheated oven for 20 minutes, then brush loaves again with egg white mixture.

9. Continue baking until loaves are nicely brown and sound hollow when tapped. Remove from oven and transfer to cool on a wire rack.

The Lone Diner

LONG AGO IN THE early days of my journalism career — when I was covering professional basketball and spending most of the year on the road with a lot of very tall and egomaniacal ballplayers and a few more egomaniacal, albeit shorter, male sportswriters — I ate a lot of restaurant meals by myself.

Not necessarily by choice. But there were rules to be followed. No fraternizing with the enemy, for one. (And I refer here to my colleagues rather than my subjects, although they, for other reasons, were taboo as well.)

Sometimes I could arrange an interview over lunch, of course. And one could always resort to the pregame pressroom, where an eclectic but prolific spread of food and a couple of chatty freeloaders could inevitably be found.

But during a game-free night on the road, when the restaurants of an unfamiliar city and my then-generous expense account lured, I frequently found myself instead ordering from room service.

Often, I just could not bring myself to make that reservation for one, ignore the raised eyebrow of the maitre d', or endure the superior glances of the women nearby, locking fingers across the table with their attractive dining companions.

For one thing, dining alone was not something I was accustomed to. When you grow up in a family with six children, the only way you are going to eat alone is if you lock yourself in the bathroom with the last of the leftover lasagna at an hour when everyone else is either engrossed in a favorite TV show or sound asleep. The dinners of my early years meant loud debates, kicks under the table, and constant reminders from Mom about manners — not the lonely sound of a fork stabbing at a solitary plate.

But midway through that first basketball season (around game No. 53), I decided I was wasting too many opportunities by hunkering down in my room. I decided to shed the cape of my insecurity and become... ta-da! The Lone Diner.

The Lone Diner would enter a fine dining establishment, look the maitre d' straight in the eye, and confidently say, "One please."

The Lone Diner would don a broad-brimmed hat slanted seductively over one eye and project an air of mysterious allure while requesting a half-order of the oysters Rockefeller, *s'il vous plait.*

The Lone Diner would never, ever, bring a book to the table. God forbid she looked that desperate. Instead, she would rest an elbow on the table and her chin on the back of her hand between courses, thinking magnificent thoughts — or maybe not-so-magnificent but more entertaining ones about the imagined proclivities of the restaurant's other patrons.

The Lone Diner would be adventurous in her food selections. She would learn to eat very slowly, savoring each bite and trying to discern individual ingredients and unusual preparations. (Good training for a future food critic).

And, eventually, she would realize that while our American culture often inextricably links eating with social interaction ("Can we meet for lunch?"), meals didn't necessarily have to be shared.

Don't get me wrong. I still feel the best part of a dinner party is that mellow time post-dessert when everyone — sated but still sipping that last swallow of wine, that second cup of coffee — is relaxed and conversational. I look forward to the nights my son joins me for dinner, both because it drives me toward more creative cooking and always rewards me with some gratitude for my effort. And what I look forward to most at my family's reunions are the raucous scenes at the dinner table, amplified by the voices of multiple generations.

But I no longer fear a meal *en seul*. Whether the lack of company allows me to admire the elegance of a starched tablecloth or a gorgeous floral bouquet at a fine dining establishment or permits me the indulgence of picking up the asparagus with my fingers at home, I now see that dining alone has its own singular merits.

And I will always remember that one evening long ago, as I sat sipping a post-dinner espresso, when my waiter re-appeared — not with the check I had requested — but instead with a bowlish glass of cordial.

When I looked up, puzzled, he smiled reassuringly and explained:

"The gentleman across the way sends this, with his best wishes."

I was tempted to ask for his name. (The gentleman's, not the waiter's — though, come to think of it, he was quite enchanting, too.)

But the Lone Diner would never do such a thing. She would want to hang on to that enigmatic air, that hint of intrigue, knowing the mystery would serve as impetus for many more solitary meals to come.

Oysters Rockefeller

*These have a sauce that is intensely rich — the name was in honor of
John D. Rockefeller, one of the world's wealthiest men at the time
of its creation — but when you're dining alone, you deserve to be
indulgent. I've also used this same recipe successfully using large
clams, harvested at low tide on one of Nantucket's beaches. It's not
traditional, but my mother added cooked crumbled bacon to the
spinach mix. That is what she used to call "gilding the lily."*

Ingredients

- 2 dozen fresh oysters, shucked and drained, with the deeper bottom shell rinsed and reserved to use as the baking dish

- Rock salt

- 6 ounces chopped spinach, stems removed and rinsed

- ½ cup butter *(1 stick)*

- 1 ½ cup finely chopped onions

- 1 Tbsp. finely minced garlic

- 2 Tbsp. sherry *(optional)*

- ½ cup cooked, crumbled bacon *(optional)*

- ½ teaspoon salt

- ¼ teaspoon freshly ground black pepper

- ½ cup cracker crumbs tossed with melted butter OR Pepperidge Farm stuffing mix

DIRECTIONS

1. Bring 1 quart water to boil in a medium pot. Add the spinach and cook until tender, 5-6 minutes. Drain spinach in colander set over a bowl to reserve cooking liquid. When spinach has cooled, squeeze out remaining liquid and finely chop. Set aside.

2. Melt the butter in a medium pot over moderately high heat. When it foams, add the onions and garlic and cook until softened, about 3 minutes. Add the 2-3 cups of spinach and reserved cooking liquid, bring to a boil and cook for 1 minute. Add sherry, salt and pepper and simmer over medium heat stirring occasionally until the mixture reduces and thickens.

3. Remove from heat, add all but 4 Tbsp. of the cracker meal or stuffing mix and combine well. (Add crumbled bacon here if you desire.) Cool completely.

4. Preheat the oven to 400 degrees. Spread a ½ inch layer of rock salt on a large baking sheet. Arrange the reserved oyster shells on top of the salt and put one raw oyster in each shell. Top with 2-3 Tbsp. of the spinach/sauce mixture, to completely cover the oyster. Sprinkle reserved crumbs on top.

5. Bake until sauce and crumbs are lightly browned and oysters have begun to curl around the edges, approximately 20-25 minutes. Remove from oven and transfer with tongs to serving plates lined with rock salt. Serve immediately.

Cookbooks

BACK WHEN I WAS in journalism school, one of my professors gave us the following assignment: interview a fellow student, someone you don't know well, and write a profile of them. Don't reveal the person's name, but be descriptive enough that we'll be able to guess who it is.

I chose a classmate who I imagined to be as different from myself as seemed possible. Catherine was statuesque, blond, and stunningly beautiful. She was the kind of woman whose hair always looked like it had just had an expensive cut and whose nails appeared never to have peeled an orange, much less touched compost or dishwater. She had that air of class, money, and privilege that is as intoxicating as it can be off-putting.

This was not a woman whom you would even consider calling Cathy.

Her father was a chancellor or dean or some other sort of muckety-muck at the university we attended. He was obviously well-bred and, like his daughter, had the impeccable manners of someone accustomed to being served dinner by waitstaff and the fastidious manicure of someone who'd never washed so much as a fork. He reminded me of the aristocratic patriarch in a novel I'd read set in the 1800s. Surely this was a family that left kitchen duty to what was referred to simply as "the staff."

So you can imagine my surprise when, during the course of interviewing Catherine, she revealed that she had an enormous library of cookbooks.

"Really?" I asked, trying hard (and unsuccessfully) to visualize her in an apron, looking a little steamy and wilted.

She confirmed I had heard her correctly. Then she went on to enumerate some of her favorites, many of which even I, a longtime cookbook collector, was unfamiliar with.

Just goes to show, I silently chastised myself, that Mom was right. You shouldn't judge a book by its cover.

"And what is it that you like to cook?" I asked eagerly, excited to have found someone with whom to share recipes and tips.

She gave me a peculiar stare and shook her head.

"Cook?" she said. "Oh, no. Why, I don't cook at all. I just like to read them."

Then she proceeded to explain how, after she'd gone through her nightly beauty ablutions, she'd pick out a choice volume, climb between the sheets (silk, I presumed) and imagine the most magnificent meals as she perused the recipes. It was easy to surmise that the pages of her cookbooks were as pristine as mine were covered with stains and spills and even bits of ingredients.

But what a fine way to drift off to sleep, I thought admiringly. With visions of rich *patés* and delicate *mille-feuilles* dancing in your head. And obviously much more conducive to maintaining a figure like Catherine's than actually making the dishes and ingesting them.

My own cookbook shelves have burgeoned further since that day, with an assortment of volumes from the homely to the exotic — gifts, review copies or just something I picked up at the bookstore after I'd buried my nose in it so long the impatient stare of the salesclerk made me feel obligated to buy something.

Taking Catherine's lead, there's nothing I now enjoy more than curling up under the down comforter for a good virtual meal before lights out.

The selection depends on my mood, my intention, my appetite. Looking for something to actually cook or just to be entertained? Imagining a perfect romantic meal or a boisterous family reunion? Something comfortably familiar or strangely exotic?

If I need a good chuckle, my yellowed, falling-apart paperback of the "I Hate to Cook Book" by Peg Bracken is sure to do the trick. Searching for something basic that my son with his one saucepan, limited funds, and impatience can manage, I take up the frugal "College Cookbook," which actually advocates buying day-old bread and past-their-prime vegetables from the discount bin.

When I'm feeling nostalgic, the plastic spiral-bound pink copy of "Favorite Recipes of Heather Hills Residents, Staff & Friends" will do. Heather Hills was the nursing home where my 95-year-old Grandma Berry lived her final days. Reading her recipe for molasses cookies with the accompanying sing-song poem brings a jolt of elementary school English class:

A house should have a cookie jar
For when it's half-past three
And children hurry home from school
As hungry as can be.

On the other hand, when I am feeling stoic, I might reach for "Escoffier: The Complete Guide to the Art of Modern Cookery," a volume so edifying I feel my IQ has risen by several points by the time my eyelids close.

It all goes to show that an appreciation of food doesn't have to begin and end with its consumption.

In fact, considering my ratty-looking hands and some of my more spectacular failures in the kitchen, I have to consider whether maybe Catherine had the right idea after all. Feasting for the eyes is ever so much more conducive to maintaining that elusive aura of perfection I've never actually been able to achieve in the kitchen.

GRAMMA BERRY'S ORANGE MOLASSES COOKIES

These are not the big, fat, squishy kind of molasses cookies, but rather delicate, crisp ones with a hint of orange (and full disclosure, this recipe comes from the Heather Hills Cookbook). They were my grandfather's favorite. (His name was Hammond, but no one called him anything but "Raz.") Note that the dough benefits from a night in the freezer, so you will need to plan ahead.

INGREDIENTS

- 1 cup butter or margarine

- 1 cup white sugar

- 1 cup molasses

- 4 cups flour

- 1 orange rind, grated

- 2 eggs

- 1 tsp. salt

- 1 tsp. baking soda

- 1 tsp. ginger

DIRECTIONS

1. Cream butter, then add sugar, grated orange rind and eggs, one at a time, and beat until light. Add molasses and

mix well. Sift remaining ingredients and add to molasses mixture until thoroughly combined.

2. Chill in freezer overnight.

3. Roll dough out as thinly and evenly as possible (⅛ inch) and sprinkle surface of dough lightly with sugar. Press the sugar in with another light roll.

4. Cut out with whatever cookie cutter shape you prefer — Gramma used a large round one with a scalloped edge — and bake no more than 10 minutes in a 350-degree oven. (Pay attention; they burn easily.) Cool on cookie rack and store in air-tight container.

Gardening in the Desert

EVERY SPRING THAT I lived in New Mexico, I would go out to the backyard strip of earth I had carved out of the mostly rock in my foothills home to plant my vegetable seeds. I called it a garden, but I seriously doubt anyone else would have.

Some seeds I dried from past crops, others were purchased at local shops, and a precious few were ordered from fat catalogues with pictures of perfectly shaped, shiny specimens that bore no resemblance to anything I would ever be able to grow.

By that time I'd already turned over the earth — with a rototiller if I'd been able to impose on the neighbor who owned one, or by the shovelful if I hadn't. I'd added and mixed in some organic material to enrich the soil. One year, it was a pickup load of dried horse manure from my family's ranch — a bargain, it seemed, until I realized horses don't digest grass seed and I had a lovely garden lawn.

I spent hours looking at the neat little diagram I arranged and rearranged on many a dreamy winter evening — carrots here, spinach there, okra (yes, I like it) in the corner. Then I'd get down on my hands and knees. And when I was done tucking the seeds in at the proper depth and width, I would turn on the sprinkling hose, look up at the sky, and pray more devoutly than I'd ever been known to do in church.

As a non-traditionally religious person, this had nothing to do with asking for God's blessings. I prayed because every year I was absolutely certain there was no possible way anything was going to emerge from the dirt without some kind of miracle.

Every day, I watered a little bit more and looked a little bit closer and became ever more firmly convinced I would not have a garden that year.

After all, New Mexico turf is hardly the soil of my childhood in Michigan — that rich blackness, so moistly fertile that if you carelessly discarded an apple core, you had automatically left a legacy of fruit for your grandchildren.

This was New Mexico, land of baking sun, rocky clay, and water-use restrictions. That a dried-up kernel of something long-ago alive should one day produce something to be served up at the dinner table seemed even too much for a Pollyanna to hope for.

And then one afternoon — seven or 10 or 14 days later — I would notice a crack in the dirt and a tiny shoot struggling to push off another rock I'd neglected to eliminate.

I could never believe it, but there it was. Something was growing.

Something, but not everything. Birds ran off with a lot of the seeds and the spring winds whisked away the lightest ones to the neighbor's yard. The year I planted soybeans, not a single one germinated. I dug them up midway through the summer and there they still were, stubbornly hard as pebbles. (And you can be sure I'll never try those again.)

But most things eventually appeared. In a few more weeks, the orderly rows I had envisioned in a winter daydream were actually visible to the naked eye, though not quite as tidy and linear as I'd imagined.

By mid-summer I'd be canning dilly beans and making zucchini bread and wondering why I thought I liked okra so much when I have now started praying for it to stop growing.

There are a lot of rewards to growing a garden; anyone who's ever tasted a vine-ripened tomato knows that much. But the rewards aren't all in the eating.

I love to count the passage of summer days by the size of a developing eggplant. I like to see a friend's gratitude at a bag of surplus cucumbers. (Notice I did not say zucchini; everyone has too much zucchini.) The canned vegetables that line a shelf in my kitchen and seem to run out just as spring reappears give me a warm feeling of accomplishment and security all winter long.

And who, save the very lazy or oblivious, would not admit that actually seeing where your next meal is coming from connects you to the food chain in a way a trip to the grocery store never could?

But nothing can quite match that first afternoon when I think I spot something on the ground: a leaf? An insect? A speck of pollen?

No, nothing much. Just a little green miracle.

CREAM OF ZUCCHINI SOUP

I made this recipe up after a friend's gift of her barely used Vita-Mix blender coincided with the usual overabundance of zucchini. It tastes rich and creamy even though it's low calorie and contains no cream and it's equally good served hot or cold. Don't worry about trying to chop everything a uniform size; it's all going to get pureed in the end, so it makes no difference.

INGREDIENTS

- 3 pounds zucchini, diced

- 2 Tbsp. butter

- 2 potatoes *(any kind will do, but Yukon Gold are creamiest)*, peeled and cut into small dice

- 1 large onion, chopped

- 3-4 cloves garlic

- 2-3 cups vegetable or chicken broth *(even water and a couple of Knorr bouillon cubes will do)*

- 1 cup whole milk

- Salt and pepper to taste

- Sour cream *(optional)*

DIRECTIONS

1. Melt butter in large soup pot; add onion and garlic and sauté over medium heat until golden.

2. Add chopped zucchini and potato, stir to mix with onions and then cover with a lid. Lift lid and stir every five minutes or so until vegetables are soft and cooked through.

3. Add broth to just cover vegetables, return lid and simmer just under a boil for 10 minutes. Add milk.

4. Remove from stove and let cool slightly. (Hot liquids in a high-powered blender can be dangerous, especially if you don't have the lid on tight. Ask me how I know.)

5. Ladle vegetables and broth in even amounts into a Vita-Mix (if you have one) or a regular blender (if you don't) and pulverize at high speed until soup becomes uniformly green and smooth. Add salt and pepper to taste.

6. Serve hot or cold; a dollop or drizzle of sour cream or plain yogurt on top is a nice touch.

Favorite Foods

QUITE SOME TIME AGO, on a road trip to I-can't-remember-where, my older sister, an excellent cook whose husband at the time lived on nothing but cheeseburgers, came up with the idea for a way to bide the time. She called it the Five Foods Game.

It's actually not so much a game as a question: if you were stuck on a deserted island somewhere for the rest of your life, what five foods could you absolutely not do without?

Here are the rules. You don't have to consider fat, cholesterol, or tooth decay in your deliberations. Your five choices do not have to be nutritionally sound at all. There is no need (unless your favorite foods actually are celery and liver) to think about roughage, vitamins, or diet. You can pick things that are out of season or grown out of the country or things that make people think you are seriously disturbed, disgusting, or boring.

You do have to be honest — even if it means admitting to an insatiable craving for chile-dusted pork rinds or chocolate-covered double-stuffed Oreos.

It's startling how hard it can be to pin yourself down to just five. What is it that you like to eat most? Could you do without ever again tasting a perfectly runny hunk of Brie, a lush, ripe strawberry, or a dense triangle of cheesecake?

Asked to play along, people will take interminable amounts of time deciding, especially with their final few selections, as if they were death row inmates debating a last meal before heading to the gallows.

"*This is hard!*" they say, accustomed to being limited by their pocketbooks, their consciences, or the contents of their cupboards.

I don't recall all of my sister's choices that first time we played, although I remember asparagus and raspberries were among them. That seemed about right. My sister is unusual without being strange, and sweet but never saccharine. She has a capacity to be both tender and tough and occasionally a little thorny. She can be abundantly generous or stingy with her affections when they aren't properly appreciated.

My own choices included a crusty, sourdough loaf and that runny Brie (no Atkins girl here), which seemed rather bland by comparison. (But then, I thought, I am rather bland by comparison!) Still, I threw in raspberries, too, and wished I'd thought of them first.

What began as a simple musing soon became a fascinating window into the person doing the choosing, a perspective that gave a whole new meaning to the phrase "you are what you eat."

For example, there was the health nut, who after listing choices like raw almonds and radicchio finally admitted to frequently devouring an entire bag of Fritos and then burying the evidence at the bottom of his trash compactor. This is a man who, on the surface, is quite perfectionistic in every way — successful in work, healthy in body, abundant in riches, meticulous in planning — but who is also addicted to "junk food" relationships that devour the women involved, whom he then casts away, covering up his misdemeanors. Fritos, you might call them.

At one point, while I was playing the game with girlfriends, a man observing nearby asked whether he could join in. Then, Scotch on the rocks in hand, he asked whether beverages could be considered food. We knew better than to follow *him* home.

It's a fascinating exercise to see what foods have power over each of us and a more telling one than we'd probably like to admit. Try it and you'll see. I'm not suggesting you choose your fiancé for his love of lobster or your personal trainer for her adoration of arugula, but you might want to run if either one mentions Ding Dongs, brewer's yeast, or freeze-dried insects.

While I am reasonably sure I will not find my soul mate in a person who lists pork rinds in his top five (then again, my father loved them, and I was very fond of him), I might find a tender spot in my heart for the sophisticated yet pragmatic someone who loves both crème brûlée and vanilla pudding.

A long time ago, I asked a young friend (who had been orphaned at age 7) to try her hand at the game. She quickly let fly her ready

favorites: Wendy's hamburgers. Curly fries. Krispy Kreme dough-
nuts.

The list left me feeling disheartened. Every item seemed to be a
reminder of the troubled, impermanent, scattered life she had led
to this point.

Then, after a long pause, she came up with her final choice. And
almost immediately, I felt better.

"My gramma's tamales," she said, nodding. "Couldn't live without 'em."

How To Assemble a Tamale

To be frank, these are a lot of work. It's best to make these when you have a kitchen crew to form an assembly line — one to soften the corn husks, one to spread the masa, one to spoon on the filling, one to close and fold the husks around the tamale, one to tie them shut, and one to load the steamer. At least, that's how we did it in New Mexico. They do freeze well (after steaming and cooling), so if you have the help, make as many as you can and next time you'll have the treat without all the assembly.

Ingredients

- Dough made from masa harina *(Maseca is a common brand)*

- Lard *(grossness, I know, but it actually has less saturated fat than butter and it's the traditional Mexican way)* or shortening *(a poor substitute)*

- Baking powder

- Broth *(beef, chicken, or vegetable, depending on filling)*

- Salt

- Dried corn husks, soaked and softened in water

- Fillings *(these are traditional, but use your imagination)*: chicken and green chile; pork and red chile; beef and red chile; bean and cheese

ASSEMBLY

1. Prepare (or purchase pre-made) your fillings of choice.

2. Prepare the masa dough (it should be the consistency of creamy peanut butter) and set aside in a bowl covered with a damp towel.

3. Lay a corn husk, glossy side up, on the counter with the wide end at the top. Place about ¼ cup of masa dough in the center and, using plastic wrap or a baggie to cover your hand to keep it from sticking to the dough, press and spread the masa into a layer about ¼ inch thick to cover the top half of the husk only.

4. Place 1-2 Tbsp. of filling down the center line of the dough. (Don't overdo it or the filling will squish out when you try to close them up.)

5. Fold in one long side of the husk over the filling and then the other side overlapping the first, so the masa is completely covering the filling. Fold the bottom of the husk up to make a neat rectangular package. Tie around the middle, like a present, with a long strip cut from the edge of a husk to keep the package from opening while steaming.

6. Add 2-3 cups water to the bottom of your stove-top steamer pot, so it doesn't quite touch the bottom of the steamer rack. Lay a few corn husks on the bottom of the rack to keep the boiling water from touching the tamales.

7. Stand the tamales upright, side by side, inside the steamer rack, so they are touching but not compacted. Lay a few soaked corn husks over the top of the tamales before closing the lid.

8. Bring the water to a boil, reduce to a simmer and steam for 1-2 hours. (Time depends on how big the batch is; you can check one in the middle after an hour. If you take them out too early, the masa will still be sticky and doughy. Fully cooked, the tamales come out of husks intact like a firm pillow.)

9. Remove tamales from steamer and serve — plain, or with sour cream, salsa, pico de gallo, etc. — allowing diners to unwrap their own. Freeze extras after cooling, still wrapped in the husks.

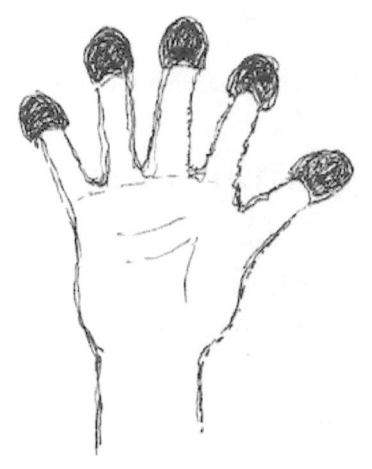

Pizza

HE STOOD IN THE middle of my small kitchen, his face set in
a stubborn grimace, his skinny arms locked across his chest.
It was a sunny summer morning many years ago now — and
probably one of the darker days of his young life.

The police had picked up 7-year-old Michael at the Central
Avenue hotel room in Albuquerque where his mother had left
him for two days without supervision and delivered him to me,
a foster parent taking emergency placements. It didn't take a
genius to see he wasn't happy to be there. The tracks of earlier
tears still showed in rivulets down his dirty cheeks, but he
wasn't about to let me see any more.

Nor was he eager to join in any activities. He remained stubbornly silent, arms crossed, eyes narrowed, brow furrowed. Finally, I resorted to what few foster children I'd known could refuse. Food.

"Are you hungry, Michael?" I asked. "What's your favorite thing to eat?"

His little buzz-cut head nodded reluctantly. Then he whispered, so softly I could barely hear him.

"Pizza."

"Would you like to make a pizza?" I asked.

He looked at me as though I were even more hopeless than he'd already surmised. Then, with not a little exasperation, he explained. You didn't "make" a pizza, stupid lady. You called on the phone, and they delivered it in a box.

"Well, did you know you can make one, too?" I suggested.

Eyeing me suspiciously, he challenged, "How?"

So, joined by my son, we got out the flour and the yeast and the biggest bowl we could find. We made a dough and mixed it with our hands. Michael kneaded his blob until it became a uniform gray.

Then, after a thorough examination of the contents of both the cupboard and the refrigerator, we assembled all the toppings we could find — tomato sauce, bacon, pepperoni, canned pineapple, black olives, and shredded mozzarella.

It was a surprise for Michael to learn that pizza didn't have to be round. We ended up with two shaped like spider webs (both Michael and my son were Spiderman fans) and one like a heart for me. ("That's stupid," Michael scoffed.)

I showed them how to spread the tomato sauce around with the back of a big wooden spoon. My son and I stuck the olives on the ends of our fingers and ate them off one by one. Michael, who had never eaten an olive, looked interested but wary. Instead, he crumbled the bacon and snitched bites when he thought I wasn't looking. Then he brazenly drank the leftover pineapple juice straight from the can when he knew I was.

Later, we sat down at the kitchen table to eat. As my son looked on aghast, Michael carefully removed every single topping from his pizza and put each in a pile around his plate. Then he systematically ate each pile and finished with the naked baked dough.

When he was done, he sat back in his chair and crossed his arms again, but this time with an air of satisfaction.

"Hey," he said. "Think we could make pizza again tomorrow?"

Michael wasn't our first foster child, but he was the first who underscored for me the power food has to create a connection, to bridge a gap in ages, cultures, or agendas.

Since that time I've made challah bread for a Christian holiday party, learned to prepare moussaka from a Greek friend's mother who spoke no English and — gingerly (and with some horror, I must admit) — tasted sheep's testicles separated from the animal by the teeth of an aged New Mexico ranch woman who roasted them over a branding fire before offering me one.

Breaking bread together becomes a way to break the ice; sharing food a way of sharing cultures, stories, beliefs, lives. The very thing that sustains us, unites us.

Long ago, in Middle Eastern cultures, it was said that those who enjoyed a piece of bread broken off a common loaf became family.

In our case, it was pizza, but it served the same purpose.

Homemade Pizza Dough

You can top this the traditional way — with tomato or marinara sauce, mozzarella cheese, and whatever else you like (pepperoni, black olives, chopped green peppers and onions, mushrooms, etc.) — or think out of the (pizza) box and use pesto or Alfredo sauce or more unusual toppings like sun-dried tomatoes, capers, or vegan meat substitutes. Some people (not me) like pineapple.

Ingredients

- 1 Tbsp. yeast

- 1 ¾-2 cups unbleached flour

- 1 cup cake flour

- 1 cup warm water

- 1 tsp. salt

Directions

1. Sprinkle yeast over ¼ cup water, warm, but not hot, to the touch. Combine flour, cake flour and salt. Make a well in the dry ingredients and pour in the yeast liquid and begin stirring, adding the remaining water as you mix until you have a sticky, thick dough.

2. Turn dough out onto a floured counter and knead for 10 minutes, adding more flour as you go if necessary, until the dough is elastic and smooth. Let the dough rise

1-2 hours until doubled in a bowl greased with olive oil; punch down and knead again briefly. Using your hands (greased with olive oil), roll, pull, and stretch the dough to desired shape; or, if making individual pizzas, separate dough into smaller balls first.

3. Place shaped dough on greased baking sheet or (preferably) an oven pizza stone.

4. Add sauce and toppings. Bake in 400-degree oven for 15-25 minutes.

The Skinny Critic

NEVER TRUST A THIN chef. Or a skinny food writer.

At least that's what people used to say when they learned I was the pseudonymously named critic for the newspaper in Albuquerque.

"You're a restaurant critic? You write about food?"

Not possible, they protested, looking at my wiry 5-foot-4 frame and hip bones that had been known to injure careless dance partners. (This was quite some time ago, I might add. Gravity has since taken its toll.)

Everyone assumes that the degree to which you love food must be reflected in the size of your jeans or the number of chins you sport. If you are not intentionally dieting and you are still slender, you must either: 1) dislike food; 2) run ultra-marathons; or 3) have a metabolic disorder.

No. No. And no. I enjoy food, exercise daily but not obsessively, have a functional thyroid, and no tapeworms.

How can this be? they ask.

When I try to convince them I remain thin because my appreciation of food might be even greater than a glutton's, their eyes glaze over, convinced that not only is my body starved but my brain cells must be as well.

Granted, I'm fortunate to have a genetic inheritance that does not predispose me to obesity. My mother, at 80, was still slender, with lovely, shapely legs. (A friend once blurted out, "I wish I could get legs like yours!" To which I replied: "I'm sorry, but I think my mother has been done having children for quite some time.") Like me, most of my siblings are small and thin. I'm lucky that way and the first to admit it.

But more influentially, from the age of 4, my aspiration was to be a dancer. And not just a dancer, but a ballet dancer. As I embarked on what I thought would become my eventual career, I learned what the ballet world had to teach me: a rigid discipline, an appreciation for aesthetics, and the reward of having a passion. And I'll admit that, for a time, that discipline, as it often does for aspiring dancers, became rather over-zealous in the food department.

That career never came to be, and my fanatic aestheticism dwindled. But the lessons carried over in a way that fueled my enthusiasm for all aspects of food.

When I am alone at home, I eat simply and with restraint. A slice of toasted homemade bread with sweet butter for breakfast, a single perfect apricot for a snack. If I do overindulge — and like anyone, I have my weaknesses — I make sure to walk an extra mile the next day. There's the self-discipline.

When I make food for others, I care as much about how it is prepared and presented, as about eating it. I like seeing the vintage wood table that once sat my entire family, oiled and set with my grandmother's old china, linen napkins, and some fragrant beeswax candles. I'll happily spend hours crafting an elaborate appetizer or fussy dessert, not in anticipation of devouring it, but in the joy of creating and serving it.

And nothing pleases me more than to have a friend say, "It's too beautiful to eat!" and then dive in lustily anyway. There's the aesthetic appreciation.

Food to me is love in edible form. That's not a new concept, but it's one that gets lost when the speed and size of a meal is a priority.

When I used to help myself to too much, my mother would say, "Your eyes are bigger than your stomach." She was scolding, but I've altered the phrase to mean that I must remember to eat with my eyes and ears and nose as well as my mouth. Instead of shoveling food in until we feel full, we should eat more fully. Feed more than your stomach, and you will assuage a hunger that can't be satiated by quantity alone.

Take a silver spoon and tap through the crystallized sugar skating rink atop a crème brûlée. Scoop a little of the cream onto the spoon and watch it quiver nervously. Draw in the scent of vanilla bean that wafts upward, the caramelly sweetness.

Then slowly, *slowly* put the spoon on your tongue and let the warmth glide down your throat, savoring the haunting aftertaste.

Ah. There's the passion.

Crème Brûlée

One of my favorite desserts and, though I rarely make it at home, not as intimidating as it sounds. A hand-held propane-fed kitchen torch will allow you to give it that perfect glacial, glazed top to cover the creamy goodness below, though you can use your oven broiler if necessary. Not for those watching their sweets, cholesterol, or weight.

Ingredients

- 1 quart heavy cream

- 1 vanilla bean, split and scraped

- 1 cup vanilla sugar, divided

- 6 egg yolks *(save the whites for your next omelet so you can feel slightly less guilty about this indulgence)*

- 2 quarts hot water

Directions

1. Preheat oven to 325 degrees F.

2. Place the cream, vanilla bean and its pulp into a saucepan and set over medium-high heat, bringing it to a boil. Remove immediately from heat, cover and allow to sit for 15 minutes. Remove the vanilla bean.

3. In a medium bowl, whisk ½ cup of the sugar and the egg-yolks until fully blended and light in color. Add the

cooled cream a little at a time, stirring constantly. Pour into individual ramekins and place them into a large roasting pan filled with enough hot water to come halfway up the sides of the ramekins. Bake until the crème brûlée sets, but still quivers in the middle, about 45 minutes.

4. Remove the ramekins from the roasting pan and refrigerate at least 2 hours. Remove them from the refrigerator at least 30 minutes prior to when you wish to serve them. Spread the remaining vanilla sugar evenly on the top of each ramekin. Using a kitchen torch (or, if you don't have one, your oven broiler on high), melt the sugar to form a crisp, caramelized top, watching carefully to avoid burning. Allow to sit five minutes before serving.

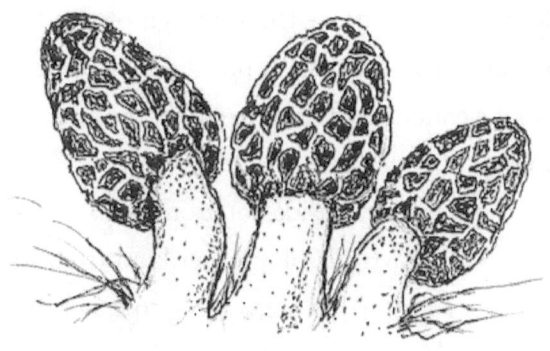

Foraging

MAYBE IT'S THE BUDS on the apricot tree in the backyard, the lengthening hours of daylight, or just the blossoming smells swirling in the gentle breezes, but something about the spring to summer season serves as a catalyst for my strongest hunter-gatherer instincts.

I can trace them back to a rural childhood in Michigan, when spring rains would produce morel and puffball mushrooms to be discovered on the long woodsy walk home from the school bus stop. Or the homesick days at summer camp when solace could only be found among the wild blueberry bushes, a berry consumed for every lonely thought.

My list of foraging memories form a map of the many places I've wandered to or settled in. In Montana, I learned to screech the car to an abrupt halt in the springtime whenever I noticed feathery fronds along the roadside — the sure sign of slender new wild asparagus shoots near the base. A hike in the Rockies never took place without a container in hand to gather the huckleberries that grew in pockets of abundance.

Visits to my parents' oceanside home on the East Coast brought a chance to forage for fruits of another kind from the sea. You couldn't be squeamish if you were going to crawl along the seaweed-covered boulders of the jetty, where the most prized mussels attached their shiny black shells like barnacles.

Nor could you turn up your nose at threading a jiggly chicken neck on a big hook to lower into the murky depths of an inlet bay. Several impatiently waited minutes — or hours — later you'd pull it up and be rewarded with the sight of a squirming, angry crab.

And if you were willing to dig your bare feet deep into the brackish mud of a tidal pool, you might be lucky enough to have your big toe jam into a monster that would win the eternal whose-clam-is-biggest family contest.

The blackberry bushes that grew in a tangled mass near the Nantucket dump were sure to leave you with scribbles of bloody scratches on your arms but also with enough "dumpberries" for Gramma Seidman's pie recipe.

Occasionally, the gods send an offering, even when you aren't focused on scavenging. I'll never forget the evening on the beachfront of a friend's Ventura, California home, when a run of grunion washed ashore near midnight, their silvery sides flickering in the moonlight, insisting on acceptance.

When I moved to New Mexico, an elderly Hispanic woman showed me where to find *quelites*, an edible weed otherwise known as lambs' quarters, that grew wild on her ranch in the northeast; then shared with me a secret for cooking them to perfection.

Of all the meals I have cooked and served and enjoyed, none have tasted better than those that came, often unexpectedly, from Earth's largesse.

Is that what drives me to rise at dawn to catch the right tidal waters, to clamber around in thorny bushes or hike, oh, just a little bit farther because the next hill might reveal a new bunch of berry-laden bushes? Or is it simply a scavenging instinct left over from cavewoman days when existence was only insured by the strength of one's drive for sustenance?

I might believe that if I didn't have so many friends who think I'm rather peculiar for wanting to spend hours plucking miniscule wild blueberries off a bush when (as they remind me) you can go to the market and get a pint of big fat ones in less time than it takes to drive to the hunting grounds.

Is it a frugality I inherited from a Depression-era mother, who cut the mold off "perfectly good" cheese and saved little bits of leftovers in containers ever-decreasing in size? Certainly the something-for-nothing aspect of gathering from the wild appealed to her.

But when I really try to dissect my passion for stalking the wild asparagus (or berry or clam), I think it comes down to nothing more complex than this: a sense of wonder and awe at an Earth we so often abuse, and almost always take advantage of, that keeps right on offering up its rich bounty nevertheless.

It would seem a sacrilege to turn my back.

Mussels and Toast Points

When we visited my parents during summers at their home on Nantucket island, we regularly gathered mussels at low tide and steamed and ate them with buttered triangular toasts made from a wonderful Portuguese bread sold at the bakery down the street. My mother called them "toast points," my then toddler son, "twoast pwoints." (And to this day, he won't eat a mussel without them.) This dish was best consumed at sunset while sitting on the rooftop "widows walk" deck of my parents' vintage home, where the wives of ship's captains used to watch anxiously for their husbands' return from sea.

Ingredients

- 4 pounds fresh mussels, rinsed and cleaned

- 2 Tbsp. olive oil

- 2 garlic cloves, minced

- 1/3 cup white wine or water

- Chopped parsley *(optional)*

- Melted butter, in copious quantity

- Good quality peasant white bread

- 1 cup butter

Directions

1. Make toast points by cutting bread into thin squares, toasting, then halving each square on the diagonal to make a triangular point. These can be served plain (as Mom did) or brushed with melted butter or garlic butter.

2. First, melt the butter and keep warm as you finish the mussels.

3. Put olive oil in heavy-bottomed pot over medium heat. Add minced garlic and stir briefly without browning. Add the mussels and stir to coat. Add the wine or water, turn heat to high and cover with led. Stir after a few minutes, then replace lid and cook until all the mussels have opened 5-10 minutes.

4. Serve mussels, surrounded by toast points, with melted butter for dipping and an empty bowl to collect the discarded shells.

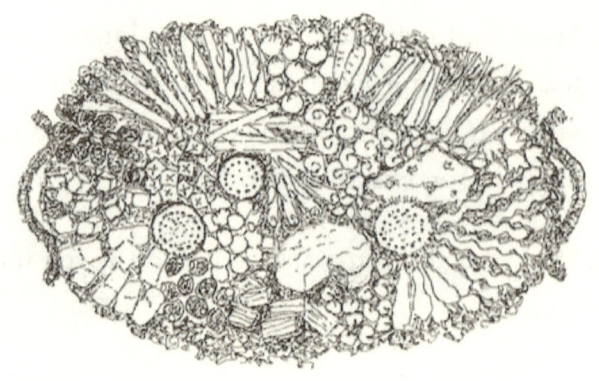

Thanksgiving

DESICCATED CORN COBS, RAW cranberries, and fake champagne. Not the usual three-course Thanksgiving lineup. But to me, those words crystallize the holiday faster and more accurately than the scent of a roasting Butterball.

Grant me a little patience. It's a convoluted story.

As in most American families, Thanksgiving in mine was a time for relatives to gather and indulge in various forms of wretched excess — eating of course, but also bizarre attire, inane practical jokes, and passive-aggressive cousin torture. Included was also the traditional bird and word (prayer).

But in keeping with the work ethic of my mother, whose Puritanical roots ran deep, you had to earn the right to eat. She felt quite strongly that Thanksgiving ought to be as instructive as it was indulgent. So it was Mom's idea to instigate an annual Thanksgiving play crafted and performed by the children before anyone could sit down to the dinner table.

This served two purposes, she felt. No. 1, it got the kids thinking about the meaning of the day. And No. 2, it got them out of her hair in the kitchen.

The theme, need it be said, was one of counting your blessings, however humble they might be.

In the early years, wary of Mom's watchful eye and limited by our as-yet uncorrupted imaginations, the play tended toward a respectful replication of the first Thanksgiving in America. A few dried-out corn cobs wrenched from the stiff stalks remaining in the summer garden served as the first supper.

But over the years, fired by the combined creative forces of siblings, cousins, foreign visitors, and the occasional bewildered but willing friend, the plays began to stray from their original solemnity and reverence.

The year Torkel — our tall, handsome, and blond exchange student from Sweden — participated, the story line was altered. Somehow it evolved into a tale of Nazis and Aryans and people racing around the supper table pelting raw cranberries at a Hitler-like figure.

Mom forbore it with a frozen smile and her customary stoicism. After all, how could she say she wasn't grateful that the world was shed of the Third Reich?

Another year the theme was "Thanksgiving in Many Lands." (I'll just let the absurdity of that sink in for a moment.) And though I don't remember the details, I know there was one rendition involving a turkey and an egg and the question of which came first.

Eventually, the string of theatrics concluded, not with a whimper, but a bang. That was the year my brother, already on his way to becoming a movie director in Los Angeles, came up with a script titled, "Just Call Joe."

The production required each of the kids in the family to play, with dead-on authenticity, the role of another child in the family in the midst of a moment of financial crisis. The solution in each case was to knock back a glass of what we called "kids' champagne" (sparkling grape juice) and "Just call Joe."

Joe, by the way, was the man who took care of my father's personal finances, the one who, at Dad's command, wrote the checks.

Perhaps needless to say, after this quite unconventional offering, the curtain was, indeed, final. But the memories of our giddy theatrics remain. And, Mom will be happy to hear, so does her intended lesson.

It's like this: sometimes what you have is a little strange, like the hearts of palm, kumquats, and pickled okra on Gramma's enormous annual Thanksgiving relish tray. Sometimes it's downright off-putting like that god-awful green Jello salad with the marshmallows and nuts the nanny made. And occasionally, it's not quite what you asked for — like a Thanksgiving play turned irreverent.

What's more important than the offering (and some things actually are more important than food) is the fact that you get to share it with the people who know you best. (And, when push comes to shove, with the dog waiting patiently at your feet.)

So when you sit down to the Thanksgiving table this year, pelt a few cranberries, kick back a glass of fake bubbly, and be grateful for the courses and the company. Then pick up the phone and wish Joe — or somebody else who's been there for you in a pinch — a very happy holiday.

Gramma Seidman's Relish Tray

Since Gramma was not a cook, this is not really a recipe, since it requires nothing but opening cans, bottles, or packages. Her ingredients came from the gourmet specialties store and there was never anything as mundane as a carrot stick or radish. Today her selection would cost a pretty penny, but if it's Thanksgiving and you can afford it, be especially grateful.

Ingredients

- Assemble the most exotic canned, boxed or bottled delicacies you can find. Here are some of Gramma's favorites:

  - Greek olives

  - Baby corn

  - Pickled okra

  - Candied kumquats

  - Marinated mushrooms

  - Hearts of palm

  - Artichoke hearts

  - White asparagus

  - Smoked oysters

- Fiddlehead ferns

- Pickled beets

- Dilly beans

- Cocktail sausages

- Tiny, shiny crackers from China in interesting shapes and colors

- Etc.

DIRECTIONS

1. Take out a large, preferably real, silver tray. Open all the cans/bottles and artistically arrange the ingredients in a pleasing pattern. In the center, place a container of tooth-picks, preferably with frilly, fringed tops.

2. Serve when the natives are getting restless waiting for the bird.

Lemonade

ON A WEEKEND DAY not long ago — one of the first truly sweat-inducing afternoons of the year — I was driving around an unfamiliar neighborhood. As I turned a corner, I saw two young girls standing beside a card table set up on the sidewalk.

"Lemonade," said the computer-produced sign on the table. Beside it was a pitcher, a stack of cups, and a glass jar.

I rolled to a stop and set the parking brake.

It had been a long time since I'd seen a lemonade stand — longer still since my siblings and I had manned our own near our childhood summer cottage in the place we lovingly called Skunk Hollow.

For us, setting up a summer lemonade stand was a vacation ritual as regular as skinny dipping in the lake or joining the library summer reading club contest. After all, there weren't a lot of other opportunities for self-employment as an 8-year-old.

I dug the loose change out of the bottom of my purse, hopped out of the truck and walked over, wearing my best "Aren't you so enterprising!" smile.

One of the girls hopped off her chair as I approached.

"What can I get for you?" she said, impressively professional for someone I judged to be somewhat shy of her first decade.

"A lemonade please," I predictably answered.

"Small or large?" she asked.

"Um... large?" I said, slightly taken aback.

"Ice?" she asked. Ice? What happened to the lukewarm liquid in the Dixie cup?

"Yeah, ice would be great," I said.

"Wanna brownie with that?" she asked, as I noticed the stack of neatly wrapped squares nearby.

"No, thanks, just lemonade," I said, clearly feeling my lack of modern day entrepreneurial sophistication.

The other girl reached for a lemon slice and hooked it over the lip of the cup. Then she handed it to me with a smile. "That'll be a dollar," she said as her friend gently nudged a "Tips appreciated" jar into better view.

I looked at the pitiful three quarters in my palm, two of which I'd intended to serve as a benevolent gratuity. Inflation was a little more inflated than I'd anticipated.

"Ah, let me just go get my wallet," I stammered.

"No problem," one of the girls said, hauling out a metal cash box. "I can make change for a $10."

I walked back to my vehicle minutes later, $2 poorer (one for the lemonade, one for the jar) and considerably surprised. This feeling was amplified after a first sip, when I realized this was not Kool-Aid or frozen concentrate, but fresh-squeezed juice. How times have changed, I thought, feeling a little nostalgic and a lot old.

Back when my sisters and I set up our summertime stands, the price was 10 cents a cup — maybe 15 if we were feeling particularly greedy or had a more expensive goal in mind. Our sign was hand-drawn with broken crayons, the juice was as warm as our fevered little brows, and if someone gave us a tip it was unexpected and never more than a nickel.

We didn't offer ice or have a cash box, unless you counted the empty cardboard egg container into which we plunked our dimes. The people who stopped to buy were neighbors we knew well, not strangers in foreign vehicles. There was no need for an adult to be posted nearby, ready to leap to our rescue should the buyer turn out to be a predator. (I guess I looked harmless enough because the woman staring out the window of the house behind the girls let them handle the transaction without interference.)

But before I could get all sentimental and old-fogyish, I watched from a discrete distance as the two girls painstakingly counted out the money in their box and their tip jar.

Then they performed an impromptu little dance, burst into giggles, and started rolling around on the lawn with their dog, leaving their table untended and the lemonade to warm in the mid-afternoon sun.

Some things never change.

LEMONADE STAND LEMONADE

Of course, these days, most kids use frozen concentrate or a powdered drink mix, if they even deign to have a lemonade stand at all. But there's no comparison with the real deal. If you happen to have a lemon tree in your backyard, so much the better.

INGREDIENTS

- 6 juicy lemons, seeds removed

- 1 lemon, sliced horizontally

- 1 cup white sugar

- 5 cups *(or more)* water

DIRECTIONS

1. Juice the lemons, which should give you about a cup of liquid.

2. In a saucepan, combine sugar and one cup water and bring to a boil, stirring occasionally, until sugar dissolves. Allow to cool. Combine the sugar syrup with the lemon juice and remaining water and stir thoroughly.

3. Serve over ice, preferably in a glass pitcher with some floating lemon slices.

Family Dinners

MAYBE, SOMEWHERE, THERE ARE families who still gather around the dinner table at night to share a meal and discuss world events.

Maybe, but I doubt it. Dinnertime isn't what it used to be, what with working parents, sports-playing kids, TV programs, and differing diets. They've all played havoc with the concept of using the dining table as a touchstone toward the end of the day.

In fact, it wasn't even a regular routine during my own childhood, though I'm old enough to have heard how that used to be the case. With a globe-trotting father, a mother known to volunteer for every organization under the sun, and five siblings with varying agendas, we didn't all gather together for much of anything, save the handing out of allowances.

But when we did, it was around a 15-foot antique pine table that was almost too long for the room and certainly too frail for the weight of family arguments that took place over it. We called these events, somewhat ominously, "family dinners." As in, "No, you cannot go to the game Saturday night. Your father will be home and we're having a family dinner."

This meant two things. One, we would be eating grilled steak and salad. Dad was a diehard carnivore and dedicated bone gnawer; Mom, equally devoted to greens, a woman before her time.

Two, this would not be a Norman Rockwell-ish kind of meal. To be perfectly honest, family dinners at our house meant someone would inevitably leave the table in tears.

OK, so it was usually me.

While the conversation at the table careened wildly in subject matter, the tone was always what you'd call (in polite company) lively. Along with sharpening your steak knife — Dad was an advocate of meat so rare it was almost still breathing — you'd do well to sharpen your tongue at our familial table. You were expected to hold your own amidst barking dogs, raised voices, clattering silverware, and inflexible biases on matters as complex as the world banking system and as obscure as an extinct species.

This was not a reserved crowd in opinion or appetite. One of my older sisters once stabbed my brother in the hand with her fork when he tried to snatch something off her plate. Another sister sprayed a waterfall of milk through her nose when the talk turned jocular just as she took a large swallow.

And who among us did not use the chaos of the raging debate to surreptitiously slide an undesirable vegetable into our napkins or under the table where the dog patiently waited for handouts, in order to clear the path for dessert?

Long after my siblings and I had gone on to create our own families and dinnertimes, "family dinner" continued to have a certain connotation to us, inexplicable and probably incomprehensible, to outsiders. The feeling wasn't nostalgia, exactly, as much as survivorship.

After a divorce, my nuclear family became smaller than any I'd ever experienced. Just two; my son and I. We folded the family table (which I'd inherited) into its smallest possible configuration and still felt dwarfed by its spaciousness.

I recall one evening when he was still in high school, we sat down to eat in a silence that felt oppressive. As was his custom, he began to shovel his food, sullenly responding, if at all, to my repeated attempts at conversation. Finally, I sighed wearily and asked, "How come our family dinners are always such a drag?"

"Because," he said with a teenager's cruelty, born of obliviousness and anger at his parents' separation many moons before, "we aren't really a family."

"What do you mean?" I protested, stung to the core.

"You know," he said, shaking his head at my refusal to acknowledge the obvious. "Family dinners means there's a mom. A dad. More than one kid. Yelling. Big bowls of food. A family."

If I'd thought it was quiet before, now the silence was deafening. I was hit by a tsunami of sadness and regret. Those were the very family dinners I remembered — with both longing and disgust —

from my childhood. That my son would never experience the same now seemed like an unforgiveable deficit.

That he would never pound on the table as angry as a hornet or sit as sober as a newly recruited AA member when something hit home. That he would never be the argumentative raised voice trying to get in that last word. That the frustration over not winning a debate would bring tears to his big hazel eyes.

But mostly that he would never leave the table with a wadded-up napkin full of lima beans, secure in the knowledge that his many siblings wouldn't rat him out.

Now that's a family dinner.

Mom's Salad Dressing

My mother was a woman ahead of her time. While other Midwest housewives were serving gooey casseroles made with cream of mushroom soup and canned or frozen vegetables, my mother served curries and stir-fries with steamed fresh vegetables. A salad was part of every meal (no iceberg allowed) and so was this simple vinaigrette, the only dressing she ever served.

Ingredients

- ½ tsp. sugar

- ½ tsp. dry mustard (today I use Dijon and more like a tablespoon)

- 1 tsp. salt

- ¾ cup olive oil

- ¼ cup wine vinegar

Directions

1. Combine all ingredients and shake well.

2. Serve with greens of any kind.

Hunger

WHEN WAS THE LAST time you were hungry?

No, not skipped-breakfast hungry or started-a-new-diet hungry or even flushing-the-system-juice-only-fast hungry. I mean *hungry* like you're not sure where your next meal is coming from — or when it comes, what it might possibly be.

I can't honestly say I have ever experienced that kind of hunger. Which is probably why I feel so guilty every time I drive past the food bank empty-handed, see a photo of a swollen-bellied child, or avoid looking directly at a gaunt-faced homeless man with a weathered cardboard sign — "Will Work For Food."

Like many people who grew up in this country during a time of great prosperity and growth, I've never had to worry about not getting enough to eat. More often, it's worrying about how not to eat too much. Pretty much every family dinner of my childhood offered a well-balanced menu of protein, greens, starch — and there was usually dessert too, if you cleaned your plate. For a long time, I didn't realize it could be any other way.

Then along about fifth grade, a new girl came to my school. Karen had frizzy, brown hair past her waist, really crooked teeth, legs skinny as the icicles hanging off our Michigan winter roof, and a wardrobe (well, actually two alternating outfits) that looked straight out of "Little Women."

It was clear her family didn't have much, but it didn't seem to have held her back. She was smart, quick, and full of an inner fire I lacked. I admired her guts in taking on the kids who teased her and envied the 100s on her math tests.

We became fast friends, though at first our rendezvous weren't equally reciprocal. Karen liked to come to my house. She liked the red licorice jar in the den, the trampoline in the yard, and the fact she got to sleep in her own bed. She liked the all-you-can-eat dinners, even when my Mom made something weird. And, for a very long time, she never returned my invitations.

Then one day, Karen's mom called mine and invited me for a sleepover. My mother never said a word in judgment as she drove me up the littered, dirt driveway to the rural, ramshackle doublewide Karen's family rented, as several feral-looking cats skittered out of her way.

"Remember your thank yous!" was all she admonished as she turned to leave.

It was about 11 a.m. In anticipation of the outing, I'd barely touched breakfast. By noon, my stomach was shrieking, but nobody said anything about lunch. Instead, Karen introduced me to the family's pet shrew, which lived in a hole in the wall in the kitchen. I wasn't sure what a shrew was, but it sure looked like a mouse to me.

Finally, Karen got hungry too and asked her mom if we could have something to eat. I watched as her mother peeled the brown skin from a big potato in one long strip and then cut what remained into thick slices and handed us a salt shaker.

I know I must have looked bewildered. We didn't eat potatoes much at our house — and certainly never raw. In fact, I wasn't quite sure this was a healthy thing to do.

I nibbled on the edge of one starchy slice as Karen wolfed down a handful. Then we went back outside to play.

The thing was, I still didn't get it. I didn't realize Karen's family ate raw potatoes for a snack because they were poor. I just thought they liked them. Ditto for the pot of beans at dinner, served with what my mother called "flannel bread," straight from the Wonder package.

When I went home the next day, I asked my mom where Karen's family came from. I thought maybe raw potatoes, navy beans, and Wonder bread were a regional specialty somewhere. And maybe they are, in that region between what a family's income is and what it costs to pay for the essentials — gas, rent, heat. My mom explained that Karen's family had far less than someone so lucky as I and I ought to be more grateful.

I felt bad but, short of saving my leftover vegetables for Karen — a plan my mother vetoed — I didn't know what I could do. I still don't.

For most of us, $4 a gallon at the pump means one fewer restaurant meal, one less sartorial splurge. It's a sacrifice, but it's not the difference between two meals a day and one. Or one and none. Yet even if I donate the cost of a full tank to the food bank, it's such a pittance it loses meaning.

Still, I put more cans in the bin at the grocery store, buy Costco-sized staples for the Boy Scouts' food drive, write a bigger check than I think I can afford.

I know it's all woefully inadequate. Because even if every time I peel a potato I remember Karen and her family, I will never truly understand what it is to go hungry.

Crispy Potato Skins

I never acquired a taste for raw potatoes. These, which require just a couple more ingredients and a short time in the oven, aren't much more difficult and give nutritional benefits from the potato skins, which might otherwise be thrown away

Ingredients

- 6 baked potatoes, insides scooped out *(and used for some other purpose)*

- 2 Tbsp. butter, melted

- 3 Tbsp. Parmesan *(or other)* cheese — or not, if you can't afford any

- Salt, pepper, garlic salt, chili powder, to taste if desired

Directions

1. Preheat oven to 400 degrees.

2. Brush the insides of the potato skins with the melted butter. Sprinkle with cheese and seasonings and, with kitchen shears or a sharp knife, cut into wedges.

3. Bake in the oven for 8-10 minutes, or until crispy and golden. (Watch carefully to avoid burning.)

4. Serve hot, immediately.

Mother Nature

BACK WHEN I LIVED in New Mexico, I could spend one day digging in my garden, getting ready to plant the sugar snaps and admiring the first pink blossoms on my budding peach tree, and the next navigating the 10-minute drive home from work, watching cars slide off the road and the world turn to an arctic fantasy land.

Ah, New Mexico, land of enchantment — and a very misunderstood climate. (This is high desert country, folks, not Phoenix, and yes, there is snow.) For someone whose favorite season is spring, who enjoys a good thunderstorm, a chance to get her hands in the dirt and even pulling weeds, it's a wonder I lasted nearly 20 years there before departing for milder climes.

I've lived in a lot of places, from my youth in Michigan to my college years in New York City to a decade in bitterly cold but utterly brilliant Montana. I even tried living in Southern California, where snow never falls and green is predominant — right along with car exhaust. I'll admit, it's hard to deny the allure of a place where the peach pit you spit out in the backyard at the end of the summer is the beginning of a tree the next spring.

But chalk it up to my New England-bred mother — who believed no job was well done unless you sweated bullets over it — the places I've enjoyed most are the ones that have dared me to take them on.

In many ways, Michigan was a paradise for growing things. Deep, rich soil; plenty of moisture; a reasonably long growing season. One of my earliest memories is of sitting in my family's vast plot (well, it seemed vast to me then, although it seemed to have shrunk enormously when I visited 20 years later) and plucking endless cherry tomatoes still warm from the sun off the vine and into my mouth.

But if I loved the garden's abundance, so did the deer and rabbits and the earwigs that annually infested the corn. And I recall more than one miserable, humid twilight spent swatting and swearing at the mosquitoes as we tried to bring in the harvest before tomato bottom rot set in or the squash bugs had devoured the zucchini.

Living in New York City, gardening meant a pot on the fire escape, moved throughout the day to catch the ever-shifting and always limited light supply, and watered with a quart canning jar filled at the kitchen sink. You knew from Day One you'd be lucky if your crop amounted to a single fruit, much less a meal.

Gardening in Montana was one of the greatest frustrations of my life and also one of the greatest rewards. You can't truly appreciate a ripe tomato if you haven't nurtured the thing from a seed started in the greenhouse in April, through the solar-heated water well housing a tiny transplant in June, to the nervous glances at the calendar in September deliberating who will win the race, you or the first fall freeze. The plants with unripened fruit, hung by the roots in the cellar next to the water heater until green turned to red, kept you in your place and appropriately humble.

In New Mexico, in addition to battling the elements, you could be plagued by your conscience every time the summertime water bill arrived. Even a die-hard gardener friend I know sacrificed her little plot one year, feeling the water consumption and effort weren't worth the miniscule payoff.

And now, in Florida, where I greedily envisioned growing the most prolific garden of my lifetime, I wage an eternal battle with my sandy, nutrition-less soil that can make water disappear like a magician; an endless assortment of diseases, insects, and predators; and a scorching sun that makes growing anything in the summertime impossible.

But I simply can't imagine missing the pleasure of picking out seeds from a catalog on a chilly winter night by the fireplace. Or watching that first tender sprout push through my sandy soil. Or that "Aha!" moment when, for a fleeting instant, I imagine I've outfoxed Mother Nature.

Once I stood on an arid ridge with a longtime New Mexico rancher, listening to him explain the elaborate watering system

— 500,000 feet of pipeline, gravity-fed, a quarter-million dollars spent and installed over years of hard labor — to produce his annual harvest.

"This country can promise you less and give you more than any country I've ever seen," he said. "On the other hand, if you abuse it, she's a long time forgivin' you."

It's a lesson every convenience-store-shopping, processed food-eating, nature-starved consumer would do well to learn and one I've reminded myself of repeatedly over a lifetime of working the soil:

Honor the promise and don't abuse the privilege.

Sarah's Fiddlehead Ferns

In my family, if you're lucky, you'll get a jar of these pickled delicacies in your Christmas stocking from my sister, Sarah, who lives in Vermont and picks the wild fiddleheads in the spring. Kids love to unwind the curled ferns, like a birthday party blower, as they eat them.

Ingredients

- 2-3 pounds fiddlehead ferns, tightly coiled and firm

- 2 cups rice wine vinegar

- 4 cups water

- 2 Tbsp. Kosher salt

- 4-5 small cloves of garlic

- Fresh dill or

- Dried dill seed and weed

- Water for blanching ferns

Directions

1. Blanch the fiddleheads by bringing a large pot of water to a rolling boil. Add the ferns and cook for just 90 seconds, covering the pot to increase the heat and making sure all the ferns are immersed. Immediately drain fiddleheads in

a colander to stop the cooking process.

2. Bring the 4 cups water, vinegar, and and salt to boil and turn off heat.

3. Drop a garlic clove and a generous amount of dill weed and seed into bottom of clean pint canning jars. Pack still warm fiddleheads tightly into each jar.

4. Reheat pickling liquid to a boil and pour it into each jar to the top, making sure all the fiddleheads are fully covered. Screw lids on jars and turn upside down to seal.

5. Jars can be processed in a quick hot water bath or simply put in refrigerator to chill.

Leftovers

"The remarkable thing about my mother is that for thirty years she served us nothing but leftovers. The original meal has never been found."

Calvin Trillin

ONE YEAR MANY YEARS ago, but for the first time in my life, I did not cook a thing for Christmas. My only child had gone to visit his father, my parents were at my brother's place in California, and my many sisters were too distant either geographically or emotionally for me to visit.

I had no excuse for a lot of kitchen bustling. I had an empty home and an even emptier refrigerator. And the saddest part of that was... no leftovers.

I found myself opening the refrigerator door periodically and, rather than admiring the cleanly spare shelves, hoping that a turkey leg wrapped in foil, some creamed onions made from Grandma Berry's hallowed recipe, or a last slice of pumpkin pie would miraculously appear. (I only encounter pumpkin pie around the holidays, which, since I like it quite a bit, seems a pity.)

I remember thinking of going out and buying a lone turkey breast and cooking it just for myself. But, to be honest, this seemed like such a pathetic, lonely-old-lady thing to do that I couldn't quite get myself to make the leap. It would have been admitting, somehow, that I had no one else to cook for, which to me, defeats the purpose of getting in amongst the dirty dishes at all.

This is a situation I now find myself in frequently. My son lives on his own now, leaving me the sole occupant of the house and the lone ranger in the kitchen. Many of my friends are coupled and busy cooking for their own partners. Without the excuse of nurturing a growing boy, foster kids, or grandchildren (I have none), I've scaled down my cooking in quantity and frequency.

Which means, when I come home late, too tired to be a kitchen queen, I'm often disappointed not to find that last homely serving of chicken enchiladas or lasagna waiting for me in its cozy little Tupperware. Dinner often becomes a hunk of cheese, a piece of fruit or, when I'm really tired, nothing at all. I've never been a convenience food kind of gal and I'm not about to start now.

I suppose I could do what those eternally cheerful women's magazines suggest and actually plan for leftovers. You know the routine: you cook a roast on Sunday, turn it into beef stroganoff on Monday, recycle it into stir-fry on Tuesday and so on and so forth, in ever more minuscule proportions, until you end up with stuffed peppers on Friday.

But, frankly, those kinds of leftovers aren't exactly a problem. In my family, if there was extra meat, what you did with it was eat it, probably straight from the refrigerator with the mayonnaise jar alongside. Or make curry (see below).

Leftovers were never an issue when I was growing up, with six siblings and an assortment of constant freeloaders filling the house. Meals were cooked in mass proportions; if you liked the result, there was always some left for the next day. And, if you didn't, someone else would probably eat it before it turned green.

Leftovers were an immutable but bearable fact of life, like homework or laundry or sharing clothes with your same-sized sisters. Sometimes they weren't exactly enticing, but their constancy was reassuring. That's because leftovers speak of more than ill-planned proportions.

They speak of generosity and abundance, and of someone at home tending the fires instead of sitting in front of a computer with a cup of microwaved ramen.

They speak of a time when everything didn't come in single-serving sizes cupped in disposable, microwaveable containers and frugality was more the rule than the exception.

And while it's hard to wax nostalgic about that new recipe that bombed and left you with an overabundance of inedible eggplant curry, there's something sad about a post-holiday refrigerator shelf that's as bare as the trees outside the kitchen window, rattling in a winter wind.

Mom's Easy (Leftover) Meat Curry

I usually make this with chicken, but it's equally good with cooked pork, beef or lamb; you could probably even use tofu. It's a simple recipe and forgiving on proportions. If you want to get all fancy, you can serve it as mom did, with an assortment of embellishments that can be sprinkled on top to taste at the table. Hers included chopped peanuts, raisins, chopped hard-broiled eggs, crumbled bacon, diced green pepper and chopped green onions. Some people like chutney with it too.

Ingredients

- ½ cup minced onion

- ½ cup diced celery

- 3 Tbsp. butter or rendered fat from cooking the meat

- 3 Tbsp. flour

- 1-3 Tbsp. curry powder *(depending on your taste)*

- 2 ½ cups vegetable or meat broth

- 2 cups diced, leftover meat

- Sat and pepper to taste

- 1 tsp. lemon juice or vinegar

- ½ cup cream or half and half

DIRECTIONS

1. Cook celery and onion until soft and golden.

2. Blend in flour and curry powder.

3. Add broth gradually and cook until mixture thickens.

4. Add meat and seasoning. Simmer 15 minutes, then add lemon juice and, just before serving, cream.

5. Serve over jasmine rice, with assorted toppings.

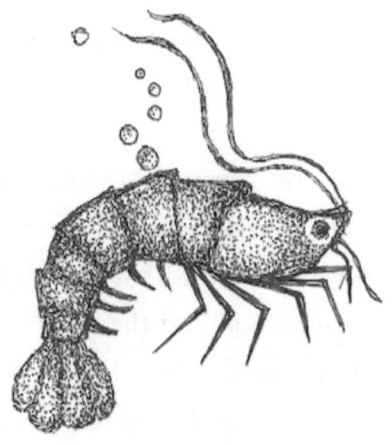

Shrimping in Sarasota Bay

AFTER I WROTE A column about an effort to put a consti-
tutional amendment on the ballot mandating Florida citizens'
right to clean water, I got a text from a former county commis-
sion candidate, Mike Cosentino, expressing his concern that
the amendment's language might be challenged by the powers
that be.

Mike, a native of Sarasota, had fought long and hard over
objections to the language in an amendment he'd proposed
— and voters approved — in 2018 to keep roads abutting
waterways open to public access. And lost.

But at the end of his message was a picture of a huge bowl of
glistening pink, head-on shrimp and a cheerier message.

"BTW, the happy part of the red tide fish kills is that the lack of predation allows a greater percentage of the juvenile shrimp to make it to adulthood," he wrote. "These are from last night in Sarasota Bay."

As fast as I could type, I replied: "I want to go!"

"Can you be ready in half an hour?" he wrote.

I couldn't, but true to his word, about a week later he offered a date when the new moon and the tides would be right. I talked about nothing else for days. My sisters, who, like me, spent Nantucket summers gathering mussels for dinner, were jealous. From everyone else, I heard a lot of Forrest Gump jokes.

Mike and his dog, Remus, picked me up in his skiff at dusk. As instructed, I was wearing water shoes and clothes "just like you were doing yard work." We motored into the Bay where the seagrass was thick and the water about knee deep. Mike set the anchor and handed me a raincoat and a headlamp.

"Can you see all of them?" he marveled. I was embarrassed to say I couldn't. "You have to look at them under your own light," he suggested, so I turned on my headlamp on and looked down. Hundreds of tiny glowing red eyes gleamed like a Christmas display. They were literally everywhere.

We tied buckets to our waists and hopped overboard holding the kind of nets on a long pole you'd use to catch butterflies. Instantly Mike began scooping up shrimp, often multiples at a time. My first few swipes were unsuccessful — those suckers can scoot and jump faster than you'd believe.

"Too fast," he counseled. "Just let them swim into your net." I did, and they did.

Once caught, you reach into the net and grab the squirming, flipping shrimp, trying to avoid the barbs on their heads and tails, and drop them through the trapdoor in the bucket so they fall into the net bag that dangles in the water below. Mike politely ignored my shrieks and squeals.

At one point, he stuck his net deep into the seagrass, hoovered it along the bottom, then lifted it up to show me the wriggling mini ecosystem within. Pinfish, spotfish, tiny shrimp with no shells, and a lot of creatures I had no name for. I tried not to think about what was slithering around my ankles.

After what seemed like 20 minutes, but was, in fact, more like three hours, a breeze came up that rippled the water, making it harder to see and we headed back to the boat to examine our haul. Mike's bag was so heavy it was a wonder his shorts didn't fall off; 10 pounds, he estimated. For a first-timer, my three pounds seemed respectable.

Glancing at the mainland, Mike said, "The people in those condos are turning down their air conditioning and I'm out here wondering if I should have brought a sweatshirt."

It was after 11 p.m. when he added, "Is it curfew, or do you have another 15 minutes?" It was so far past my bedtime 15 minutes wasn't going to make much difference, so I said sure. With which he set a pot on a small gas camp stove, dumped two handfuls of shrimp with just the water on their bodies in, and covered it with a lid.

A few stirs and a couple of minutes later, we were inhaling shrimp like whales eating krill, tossing heads and shells overboard. Mike, who has explored these waters since childhood, regaled me with stories of fishing and diving for lobster in the Keys. Then we fell silent, taking in the new moon, the night sounds, and the gentle rocking of the boat while the sweet and salty essence of the sea lingered on our tongues.

One shrimp — a monster — remained in the pot. "Please," Mike said, nodding for me to take it. I did, if only to make the enchanted moment last.

Minutes later I was waving goodbye, wading back to shore with my catch in an empty dog-food bag. At home, I rinsed the shrimp off and stuck them in the refrigerator to clean and freeze in the morning. Despite the hour I couldn't fall asleep, remembering the joy of the hunt, the beauty of the Bay, and the wonder of the sea's bounty.

The next day, I texted Mike another thank you. His reply took the words right out of my head.

"I have to think if more people knew about the 'real' Florida, they would be more proactive about preserving and protecting it."

Marinated Rosemary Shrimp

Nothing will ever taste as good as those shrimp I ate, cooked without a single other ingredient but seawater, at midnight, in the moonlight, while bobbing on the Bay. But this is another simple family recipe, which can be served hot or cold, for another day.

Ingredients

- 2 cloves garlic, minced

- 2 Tbsp. minced fresh rosemary leaves *(or 1 Tbsp. dried)*

- ½ cup dry white wine

- 2 Tbsp. fresh squeezed lemon juice

- Salt and pepper to taste

- 1/3 cup olive oil

- 1 pound medium shrimp, shelled

Directions

1. Combine first four ingredients, add salt and pepper.

2. Heat oil in large pan, then saute shrimp for 3 minutes or until pink.

3. Combine shrimp with liquid mixture and allow to marinate, in a single layer, for one hour, or overnight.

4. Can be served cold as an appetizer, on a bed of assorted greens as a salad, or reheated and served over pasta.

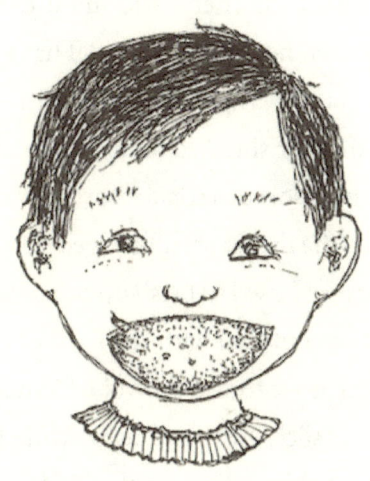

Playing with Your Food

ONE OF THE JOYS that disappears as we mature in our eating habits is the pleasure of playing with our food. I was reminded of this the day I was visited by a young friend who asked if she could have an orange from the bowlful on my table. I reached for one and stuck a fingernail in to initiate the peeling.

She looked stricken.

"No! Don't!" she said, all manners discarded in her concern. "I want smiles."

It took me a few seconds to remember what she meant — long enough to recall holding quartered oranges in my front teeth, closing my lips over the section, and revealing "monkey smiles" to my sister.

"Ya's bebber," my little friend said minutes later, the hunk of rind jammed between her lips, garbling "That's better."

There was no way I was going to repeat the "Don't play with your food!" my mother shrieked almost daily at her six children, even though I'm now sort of a stickler for manners myself. Because all at once, I was in the throes of full-fledged nostalgia... remembering how my sister and I used to mash up our cottage cheese (which we actually liked very much) with the back of our forks and take turns making faces as we forced down our "squash."

Or how we stole slices of the squishy white loaves my mother referred to as "flannel bread" from the kitchen at summer camp and mashed them between our thumb and forefinger to make doughy "bread balls."

How the only proper way to eat an ice cream cone was to bite off the tip and suck from the bottom. Or that eating a spaghetti noodle required inhaling until the strand disappeared with a satisfying "smack!" against your lips.

Delia Ephron — who, like I, will forever live in the shadow of her gifted older sister — wrote a wonderful book called *How to Eat Like a Child*. In it she details how to discretely cough food into your napkin when it displeases you or how to properly munch an animal cracker (legs, head, body).

There is an undeniable glee in making butter swimming pools in mashed potatoes, sticking black olives on the ends of your fingers, and dividing spinach into infinitesimal piles (to avoid eating it). Even though we know (I can hear it still) "You mustn't play with your food!"

It recalls a time in life when food was free from the tyranny of social convention, when you could say, without editing or embarrassment, "Yuck, I don't want that," instead of (as my grand-mother counseled) "I've had sufficient." And you didn't think twice about picking that slimy okra out of the gumbo, if you even deigned to try the gumbo at all.

I'm not suggesting children should be encouraged to be unman-nered, finicky, or allowed to chew with their mouths open. But to take pleasure in blowing bubbles through a straw on a hot day or refusing to join the "clean plate club" creates for them a happy relationship with food, free from the obsessions and self-induced deprivations that too often come later.

To this day, though he is now an adult (chronologically anyway), two of my son's favorite foods are string cheese and "open-up peas" (English peas, shelled and eaten raw). And part of why he loves them is because they are fun to eat. They require him to peel and pop and to actually think about what he is putting in his mouth. He likes the interactive involvement, not to mention his own nostalgic memories of downing peas at the farmer's market as a toddler.

So, every once in a while, maybe when no one is looking, go ahead and play with your food. Remember how much better that fresh asparagus tasted when you didn't have to fight it with your knife. Better to indulge with joyful abandon from convention than with guilt.

Gramma Berry's "Scramble"

This is strictly a finger food snack, and a rather addictive one, I might add. (The recipe makes a massive amount.) Others call it "Chex Mix," but in our house it was always "scramble," because that's what we all did when Gramma showed up with a jar of it. It inevitably provoked arguments and charges that someone was picking out "all the good stuff," but if you can find a balance between those who go for the nuts and those who prefer pretzels, it might all even out.

Ingredients

- 1-2 pounds mixed nuts *(depending on how much you like nuts)*

- 1 12-15 oz. box each: Cheerios and corn, wheat and rice Chex cereals

- 1 bag pretzels, slim sticks or small bites

- 2 cups vegetable oil

- 2 Tbsp. Worcestershire sauce

- 1 Tbsp. garlic salt

- 1 Tbsp. seasoned salt

Directions

1. Mix everything together in the biggest bowl you've got.

2. Spread on in a layer on baking sheets and cook in a very slow oven, about 250 degrees, for two hours, turning over with a spatula every 15 minutes or so.

3. Allow to cool and store in a moisture-proof container.

Soup & Popcorn

AFTER THE 13 FAMILY members I hosted for a holiday dinner were on their way home and Grandma's good china was washed and put away, I filled my biggest stockpot with water, put the turkey carcass inside, and set the burner on a low flame.

Then I curled up on Grandpa's old lounge to read my new food book and wait for the meal I was anticipating more than the one I'd just had.

Heaven, I thought sometime later, as the pot began to boil and a heady smell invaded the air. Soup's on.

Anyone who's dined out with me will tell you that soup is a mainstay of my diet. I have been known to make an enormous pot of split pea soup and a loaf of challah on a Sunday and dine on it for the rest of the week without a moment of remorse or tedium. I eat chicken soup with matzoh balls when I am perfectly healthy, as well as when I have a cold; I've been known to choose vichyssoise over Cream of Wheat for breakfast.

And what I prefer to eat with my soup is popcorn.

That's because Sunday nights in my childhood were soup and popcorn nights. Mom, an excellent cook but understandably, with a brood of six, weary of the dinner grind, took Sunday night off. Our meal was a bowl of soup she'd made in advance and put in the freezer (Campbell's was inferior and extravagant, she maintained), and a huge wooden salad bowl full of popcorn with generous amounts of butter and salt.

This we kids were allowed to eat while sitting on the floor in "the den," a room most noted for its actual pigskin floor and for a seductive jar of red licorice on the desk, the only candy in the house.

Oh, and also the television.

Any other night of the week, TV watching during meals was forbidden. We sat at the antique table in the dining room, and when rivalrous conversation had deteriorated to stony silence, looked out on a backyard full of chickadees, snow sculptures, or lilies of the valley. Or surreptitiously peered under the table for the one dog who would eat our rejections.

But, ah, Sundays. Then we were allowed to sprawl on the floor in front of the TV, wrestling over the bowl of popcorn that Mom kept replenishing and slurping our soup in a way highly unaccept-able at any other time. ("Dinner is to be eaten, not heard," as Mom would say.)

And while we ate, we watched our favorite programs. Programs like *Walt Disney's Wonderful World of Color*, with its burst of paint box brilliance in the title sequence. And *The Ed Sullivan Show*, with its wooden host — a former newspaperman who taught me early on some journalists ought to stay in print. My favorite was *The Smothers Brothers Comedy Hour*, with its razor-edged jokes that gave me my first political sensibilities and censorship problems that bred my staunch First Amendment beliefs.

There was something comforting about this ritual, from the informality and disregard for manners to the warm satisfaction of those steaming bowls of soup. To this day, on a night when I'm feeling in need of nurturing, I get a craving for soup and popcorn.

This year's holiday turkey became green chile turkey soup and turkey soup with mushrooms and barley and, finally, turkey soup with homemade noodles. The freezer is full for more than a month of Sundays.

So last Sunday when my son, sick with a cold and bronchitis and watching TV wrapped up in a blanket on the floor, asked for something to eat, I suggested some nice hot turkey soup.

"Ad bobcorn," he added stuffily.

Chicken Soup with Matzoh Balls

Despite my Jewish ethnic heritage, I never had a matzoh ball until I was well into adulthood and had to teach myself to make this version of the classic. I had to teach myself to make Challah bread too and if I'm feeling really kitchen ambitious, I make both to enjoy what I consider a perfect meal.

Ingredients

- 3 quarts chicken stock *(make it from simmering the bones of a store-bought rotisserie chicken and you'll have the cooked chicken you need too)*

- 3 carrots, peeled and chopped *(I make them into half moons)*

- 4 stalks celery, chopped

- 1 large onion, chopped

- 1 cup diced chicken, light or dark meat

- 6 oz. fideo, or very fine noodles, cooked separately

- Salt and pepper to taste

- ¾ cup matzoh meal

- 3 eggs

- 2 Tbsp. vegetable oil or melted chicken fat *(schmaltz)*

- 1 Tbsp. chopped dill

- 2 Tbsp. broth or water

DIRECTIONS

1. First, make the matzoh balls by whisking the eggs in a bowl. Add the oil or schmaltz, broth, dill and matzoh meal to make a soft dough. Cover and put in the refrigerator.

2. Place broth and all the vegetables in a large stockpot. Bring to a boil and then reduce to a simmer and cook for at least ½ hour. Add meat and cooked fideo and reduce to lowest heat.

3. Bring a saucepan of water to boil; reduce to simmer. Remove the matzoh mix from the refrigerator. Scoop out a generous tablespoon full of the mix and shape it into a ball with slightly damp hands; repeat until you've used up all the mixture. Drop balls into hot water and cover with lid, simmering at least 10 minutes until they have expanded and are cooked through.

4. Ladle the soup into bowls and place one or two matzoh balls in each. Serve hot.

S'mores

ONE OF THE RESULTS of writing about food for a newspaper is you are deluged with spam, catalogs, press releases, and come-ons from every food-related merchandiser in existence.

Sometimes this is quite enchanting. I admit to spending far too many minutes marveling over tiny jars of caviar that cost more than my weekly salary or dreaming of the day when my kitchen, too, will be outfitted like Jacques Pepin's.

But the other day, I opened a catalog and thought, "OK, now you've gone too far." There it was, on Page 27: a "s'more maker."

"Why bother with a campfire?" the ad read, "when you can have tasty, authentic s'mores at home in minutes?" The picture showed a miniature hibachi grill, heated by Sterno (not included), over which you would toast marshmallows held with little tongs.

"Well," I thought, "isn't that something?" They'd managed to take both the "outdoors" and the "kid" out of the quintessential kid's outdoor treat. Now you could sit on a kitchen stool and never once experience the dubious rush of watching your marshmallow burst into a blue flame and drop into the embers.

I'll admit, being a fan of neither chocolate nor marshmallows, s'mores weren't something I craved as a child. But I would never have passed up the yearly ritual I associated with them.

During every summer of my childhood spent at our cottage on Lake Michigan, the neighborhood kids put on a play. Well, we called it a play, but it really consisted of lip-syncing the words to *The Music Man* or *Camelot* on my family's back porch as the record player blared out an open window.

We'd line up a couple of dozen chairs for our audience, each member of whom was charged 10 cents. Mostly it was parents, but one memorable year it was the director of the local summer stock theater who paid his dime, laughed until tears fell down his cheeks, and told us we were all destined for greatness. (Of course, we believed him.)

The whole reason for our thespian philandering was to earn enough money to lay in a large stock of s'more makings for our annual sleep-out on the beach. When the chosen night arrived, we gathered driftwood to make a huge campfire, gorged to a state of near-nausea, washed off with a midnight skinny dip, and swore never to eat a s'more again. Somehow, the aversion always turned to anticipation by the following summer.

Even though I didn't especially like eating them, I loved the challenge of toasting a fat marshmallow to an even and crispy brownness over the open flames. In all modesty, I must admit I excelled at this and callously sniggered in superiority as I watched my siblings' less patient efforts go down in flames.

Which is why the idea of this s'more maker bothered me so much.

And that wasn't the only thing. Turning the pages of the catalog I found a "cuber" that would make short work of Mom's tutorial on how to dice a hard-boiled egg in the palm of your hand and a chestnut roasting pan that could single-handedly change the lyrics to the age-old Christmas tune. There was even a "modern" Danish Ebleskiver iron. (I have no idea, but it was obviously something to make your ebleskivering less onerous.)

I once saw an episode of the cartoon show *The Jetsons* in which the space-age family pushed a button on an appliance and an instant meal appeared. As a child, I thought: Cool, maybe that will happen in my lifetime.

Now, it nearly has. You can dump a bunch of flour and water into a plastic box and have a loaf of bread a few hours later. You can buy an oven/refrigerator that saves you the effort of moving your TV dinner from the freezer or turning a gas knob.

And somewhere some little girl is going to grow up making s'mores over a can of Sterno, rather than holding a whittled branch over a dancing driftwood fire while waves slap a steady drumbeat along a shoreline.

S'MORES THE OLD FASHIONED WAY

We still make these when we gather with the grandkids, now scattered from British Columbia to London, for our summer reunions. Since I don't like chocolate or marshmallows, for me it's all about the kids' enjoyment and my own childhood memories. These are excruciatingly sweet, so be prepared for some sugar-rush meltdowns.

INGREDIENTS

- Graham crackers, broken into squares *(halved)*

- Full-size marshmallows

- Hershey's chocolate bars, broken into squares to fit the crackers

DIRECTIONS

1. Build your campfire and let it die down until there are still flames, but it's not too hot to get close to. Meanwhile, send the older children out to gather green sticks they can whittle to a point on one end with a dull knife. Deliver dire warnings to those who are compelled to use these sticks as swords.

2. Place a marshmallow firmly on the end of each stick and allow the children to roast their own over the open flames. Wipe away tears and reload with fresh marshmallow when someone's bursts spontaneously into flames and falls into the coals. Meanwhile, place a square of chocolate on each

half graham cracker. When a marshmallow is cooked to preference, place it (still on the stick) on top of the chocolate, place another graham square on top of it and squeeze together the two sides of the "sandwich" while the stick is pulled out.

3. Eat immediately. Reload and repeat until everyone has had so much sugar the inevitable tantrums begin.

Holiday Cookies

IT'S THAT TIME OF year when I buy flour in a 25-pound sack, replenish my supply of red food coloring (why don't the other colors ever run out?), and get five yellowed and crusted cards written in my mother's perfect slanting penmanship out of the recipe box. Like an addict inexorably drawn to what is craved yet also abhorred, I add to a schedule already packed with work, classes, wrapping, and shopping the labor of crafting assorted Christmas cookies for gifts, as my mother did throughout my childhood.

The recipes are always hers and always the same. Frosted cutouts in holidays shapes, nut balls, spritz, toffee cookies, and meringue wreaths. The cutters and cookie press, which I inherited after a severe stroke left her with only one able arm, are hers too. So is the intention; to her mind, something homemade was always better than anything store-bought.

My back aching as I bend over the kitchen counter, meticulously painting a snowman's tiny carrot nose with a fine-bristled paintbrush as she did, I wonder why I am compelled to repeat this ritual every year right down to the three strategically placed cinnamon imperials representing holly berries on every single meringue wreath. Why does skipping even one step feel like cheating?

Part of it is sheer nostalgia... Five little girls powdering the kitchen with flour, turning soft, butter-colored dough into tough, grimy, gray balls. The smell of burning sugar from an excess of colored sprinkles. Fragile cookies shattering when pudgy hands handle them clumsily. Tears averted when Mom calls out: "It's all the same to your stomach!"

Then it's Christmas Eve, and we're going to that annual party at the Sawyers' house that we hated because Mr. Sawyer was always sloshed and squeezed us a little too tight for a little too long. Afterward, we would drive around town, taking turns running up treacherously icy sidewalks to ring doorbells and deliver the cookies to family friends.

Later, in front of the fireplace in our pj's, Mom would read "The Night Before Christmas" and help us write a note to Santa to go along with the cookies we'd reserved for him. We always tried to pick out the best ones, but the best ones were always Mom's.

In the morning, we would find a note from Santa in a contorted script that looked like it was written by someone trying to disguise their handwriting. He always complains that we are making him fat, but the year we leave skim milk instead of the eggnog Mom forgot to buy, we judge the presents as not quite up to snuff.

But back to the present. Here it is 2 a.m., and I am still hunched over the dining room table, painting perfect stripes on candy canes, waiting for the meringues to harden in a slow oven and feeling my bubbly Christmas spirit beginning to dwindle. Why do I do this?

Maybe it's the comfort of routine. You decorate the tree. You hang the wreath. You bake the cookies.

Maybe it's because I've done it for so many years now that my friends have come to see the arrival of the cookie plates as an essential part of their own holiday rituals, as Mom's did.

For a half-terrifying moment, I think it's because the one thing I swore would never happen in this lifetime has, in fact, occurred: *I have become my mother.*

Obviously, the Earth would not stop rotating if I decided to discontinue the tradition. The decorations would still come and go, Pillsbury would still be in business, and I wouldn't be out of red food coloring when it came time to dye the Easter eggs.

But there's something about the continuity: a hand-printed recipe card greasy with the fingerprints of several generations of bakers; a cherished cookie cutter worn from pressing the same shape into the dough for the 100th time; a lone baker laboring into the wee morning hours to give a handcrafted gift.

Yet it's more than just that. Wrapped up in this aggravating but cherished ritual is every lesson Mom ever taught us:

Take pride in your work. Finish what you start. Be faithful to friends and traditions. Give to others in a meaningful way. Clean up your mess.

And when the cookie crumbles, laugh it off. It's all the same to your stomach.

"Cut-Out" Christmas Cookies

This recipe card from my collection is so old and stained I can barely read Mom's handwriting. But it doesn't really matter since I know it by heart, anyway. What made Mom's version particularly noteworthy was her artistic prowess in hand-painting the cookies with frosting. I don't have her talent or her patience, but I do have her cookie-cutters. And I still use a paintbrush, if not with as much finesse.

Ingredients

- 3 cups unbleached flour

- ½ tsp. baking powder

- ⅛ tsp. salt

- 1 cup butter

- ½ cup sugar

- 1 egg

- 2 tsp. real vanilla extract

Directions

1. Mix dried ingredients and set aside. Cream butter and sugar thoroughly. Mix in egg and vanilla. Stir in flour mixture to create dough. For easier handling, chill in refrigerator or freezer for at least 1 hour.

2. Roll out on a floured surface as thinly as possible. (This creates the best dough to frosting ratio). Cut out using Christmas cutters and use spatula to transfer to greased cookie sheet.

3. Bake in 350 oven for 5 to 10 minutes. (If they are very thin, they won't take long.)

4. Transfer to wire rack to cool. Frost with a confectioner's sugar icing, tinted different colors with food coloring, using a paintbrush or, if you're lazy, a knife. Allow frosting to dry before placing in container or cookie jar.

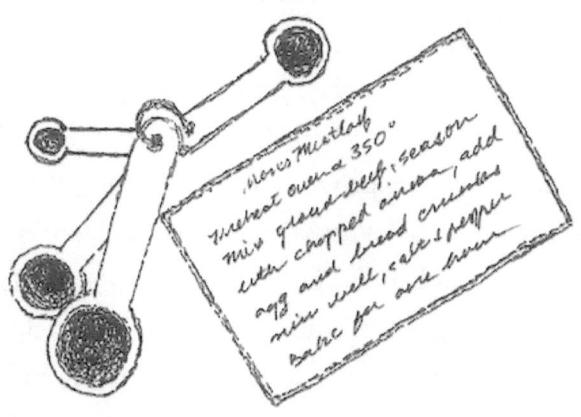

Family Recipes

WHEN MY SON TURNED 21, for this most significant and momentous birthday, he asked for just one thing: my recipes.

Contemplating a life that didn't include Mom doing his laundry and eating fresh-baked bread, he decided he'd have to learn to create for himself what until now he's always been quite content to have me make for him.

Now, one might imagine that the son of an avid cook would have a good number of culinary skills already. Unfortunately, one would be mistaken. Because I like to cook and because he often was more interested in playing on the piano or with the cat when I was cooking dinner, his expertise in the kitchen is far short of basic. Since his learning disabilities make it hard for him to follow recipes, he's taken to watching YouTube videos, with cooks who have more patience than his mother in tediously explaining every step.

If you need someone to shell fresh peas, he's a whiz, though there's not likely to be enough left for dinner when he gets through. He can knead dough to a remarkably resilient consistency — something akin to Silly Putty, remembering only afterward that he forgot to wash his hands. The first dinner he ever made for me by himself — a "magic crust" quiche made from the recipe on the side of the Bisquick box — will remain forever in my mind as the most appreciated of the unfortunate tasting meals of my life.

Regrettably, I never taught him to make a vinaigrette, flip an omelet, or whip egg whites. So when I pulled out my tattered array of old recipe cards to put something together for his birthday, I was forced to reinterpret each one in the eyes of someone who has not memorized half *The Joy of Cooking* and cannot measure a teaspoon in the tight cup of his palm.

Each yellowed card brings a remembrance of my own path to kitchen prowess. The one from my mother for blender-crafted mayonnaise uses raw eggs that would be scorned today for their salmonella potential. It doesn't say "mayonnaise" at the top but rather "mayonnaie," followed by an asterisk and an explanation. That's the way my younger sister copied it down long ago and Mom never had the heart to correct her.

There's the grease-stained copy of my first boyfriend's mother's favorite casserole, a chicken/broccoli "divine." (I assume this was supposed to be "divan" but in her vocabulary, a divan was a pull-out sofa for accommodating unexpected overnight guests.)

I once read an article in which this woman's husband was asked what his favorite dish was. "Everything my wife cooks," he said, a response that was honest rather than dutiful. Like most Midwestern 1950s housewives worth their salt (and quite a bit of salt it was), she relied heavily on canned soups; this particular casserole calls for two cans of cream of mushroom and a half-cup of Miracle Whip besides. Remarkably, she is still alive today.

One day, a woman I was interviewing for a story baked a carrot cake on my behalf and sent most of the enormous piece she cut home with me. I wrote her a note of thanks gushing about the treat and by return mail received three microscopically scribbled cards, a recipe so meticulously detailed even my son would have no questions. That one's in here too.

Then there are quite a few that I clipped or copied or asked for because they sounded simple or interesting or just plain weird but never got around to making. Chicken thighs with olives and prunes. "Trailer Park Hash." Turkey jerky.

I took a long time narrowing down the selections to my son's favorites and trying to erase my assumptions and write each one for a novice. "Take out a medium saucepan." (Do I have to explain what a saucepan is?) "Brush lightly with olive oil." (Will he know I'm referring to a pastry brush?) Then I copied them carefully by hand, startled when I noticed how eerily similar my penmanship is to my mother's.

Of course, it would have been simpler, faster, and even neater to do this on the computer. But somehow, that seemed wrong. It would make them something manufactured, something not "Mom's Recipes" as I carefully lettered the cover.

Someday when I am decrepit and demented or just long gone, I like to think of my son pulling out this book and remembering how good the house smelled when the challah was baking or how happy he was when I said his favorite, "pork chops," when he asked what was for dinner.

Then perhaps after his son or daughter has carefully clipped the top of each leaf with the scissors, he'll steam a fat artichoke and whip up a little mayonnaie to go with it.

"Mayonnaie"

Yes, this recipe contains raw egg, which these days is a no-no. That said, I have been eating it all my life and yet... well, here I am, still. It's not as economical to make from scratch as it once was — and of course, more work — but if you've never had homemade mayonnaise, it's well worth a try.

Ingredients

- 1 egg

- 2 Tbsp. vinegar

- ½ tsp. dry mustard

- ½ tsp. salt

- 1 cup salad/vegetable oil

Directions

1. Combine first four ingredients in a blender. Turn the blender on medium low speed and add the oil in a thin stream, very gradually; the mixture will thicken as it blends. Pour into a jar and place in refrigerator, where it will thicken a bit more. (Because it has no emulsifiers or artificial ingredients, this mayonnaise will be thinner than the store-bought variety.)

Christmas

MAYBE IT DIDN'T HAVE anything to do with the fact that we had
prime rib that Christmas Eve instead of the traditional turkey. But
in a child's mind, it was easy to imagine something so insignificant
as the catalyst for everything that came after. Looking back, I
remember it as a turning point of my younger years — a moment
when nothing that came after was ever again so innocent, carefree,
or limitless as it had been before.

I don't remember how old I was; I'm guessing maybe 11 or 12.
I know we were still celebrating Christmas Eve as we always had
before, with a big dinner at my father's only sister's house. But that
year, Aunt Nancy had a new husband. And from the looks of their
spacious new house on Wealthy Street (I did not make that up), he

was rich. He was an acquaintance of my father's and, like my dad, his name was Bill.

At any rate, this year the holiday seemed full of prosperity, plenitude, and possibility. The tray of exotic hors d'oeuvres from the specialty shop my grandmother brought every year — things like hearts of palm and candied kumquats and pickled okra — seemed vaster than ever. My mother, who made the best pie crusts ever, outdid herself on dessert. And then there was that roast: garish in its size and the blood-red drippings that pooled under its enormity.

Downstairs, there were what seemed to be hundreds of presents under a giant tree. Upstairs, my four cousins each had a bedroom — something that made me, who shared a room with a slobbish and bossy sister one year older, incredibly jealous. It was to one of the multiple bathrooms upstairs that four of us "middle girls" retreated after my cousin Mary Esther (named after Gramma) filched a pack of unfiltered cigarettes from her mother's purse while the dinner preparations were in full swing.

Sitting on the edge of the tub, my precocious younger cousin expertly knocked a single cigarette out of the pack and handed me a match.

"Not like that, you idiot," Mary said, as I held the flame to one end as if I were lighting a candle. "Like this."

She jammed one end between her lips, took a long draft, cocked her jaw, and blew out a stream of perfect little o's. I was enchanted. Also uninformed. After one tentative puff, I gagged, choked, spit, and felt very close to tossing my undigested hearts of palm.

Eventually, there were footsteps on the stairs. Pounding on the door. A futile scramble to hide the evidence and waft away the haze.

My aunt, with her usual classy style, handled the whole thing with equanimity. I can't remember her words, but I do remember that, without ever raising her voice, she made us feel like we didn't deserve any kind of Christmas at all. Possibly ever.

We slunk back downstairs. Even Gramma wrinkled her nose when we entered the room — as she was known to do when something was extremely distasteful to her. It was the same look she'd displayed when she came to pick up my sister and me for lunch and we hadn't showered after finishing our horseback ride. It was the first time I can remember feeling truly bad on the Christmas holiday.

Uncle Bill — though we couldn't bring ourselves to call him that because he was so new to us — carved the beef. It tasted strange, maybe because it wasn't turkey, but more likely because it didn't go well with a side of shame. In fact, whether it was the menu, the setting, or the smoking, everything tasted different that year. And Christmas Eve was never quite the same again.

Because the next summer, as I was getting ready to go down to the beach at our summer cottage, the phone rang. "It's for you, Dad," I said, handing him the receiver and waiting, as usual, to eavesdrop. He answered, and for the first time I can recall, he was speechless. His face went white.

Hanging up the receiver, he whispered to my mother: "Bill's dead. He shot himself."

Half a dozen years later, I got a similarly breathtaking call. "Aunt Nancy's gone," my sister said.

It wasn't a bullet this time or a surprise; she'd been diagnosed with leukemia the year before. But the shock was the same. It was another of those dark impossibilities that hadn't been fathomable before that long-ago Christmas Eve. That year of no turkey.

Stuffing, with or without the Bird

My father, a man who thought anything inside a sausage casing was the best thing one could eat on any occasion, used to put sliced bratwurst into this mixture, which we all found appalling and which I do not recommend. However, you can add in or leave out anything you do or don't like — sautéed mushrooms and black olives are a regular addition to mine.

Ingredients

- ½ pound ground sausage meat

- 2 cups chopped onions

- 2 cups chopped celery

- 8 cups toasted or stale bread, broken into small pieces

- ½ tsp. salt

- 1 tsp. ground sage

- ½ tsp. rosemary

- Freshly ground pepper

- ½ cup chicken or turkey broth

Directions

1. In a frying pan, brown sausage meat. Remove the meat, leaving the rendered fat in the pan and saute the onions

and celery in the fat until tender.

2. Put the bread crumbs/cubes in your biggest bowl and toss with the meat, onions, celery, and seasonings (and any other additions you like), moistening to preference with the broth.

3. This can be cooked inside the cavity of a turkey, or in a separate casserole dish (in which case, add a bit more broth to keep it moist).

Toots

Everybody eats. Therefore, everybody farts.

Hard as my mother tried to convince us kids that flatulence was not only uncouth, but unnecessary, the truth is all things must pass. And sometimes those things are audible and aromatic.

Even though my mother has been gone for nearly 15 years, I can visualize her squirming right now with disapproval and discomfort. This is not a subject to be discussed at all — *much less in a public forum!* I hear her say. Meanwhile, I can hear all my grown siblings giggling.

In our household, using this "f-word" was more perilous and punishable even than saying "Shut up!" to your sister. So we came up with euphemisms like "poof." One of our Great Danes, best known for his contributions to the atmospheric ambience, came to be referred to simply as "Phooo."

Having since had an ex-husband who was fond of asking his toddler son to "Pull my finger," and various boyfriends who proved their manliness with the decibel level of their blasts, I know that not everyone grows up with such restrictions and inhibitions. Which makes me wonder sometimes if Mom didn't do us a disservice.

Because of this attitude of... um... repression during our impressionable years, I and my five siblings — even now as elderly fuddy-duddies — find the entire subject of "breaking wind" cause for uncontrollable mirth. It takes but a mere squeak to send us into gales of giggles — to the extent that our own much less repressed children are frequently appalled by our immaturity.

There is a TV commercial on right now for a gas-reduction product in which a gentleman is giving a presentation and his every other word is a metaphor for internal combustion. The gist of the message is this: The more you try to squelch something, the more it asserts itself. Perhaps if we had grown up with a more blasé attitude about the body's natural functions, incidents would not occur like this one I remember from my younger years.

It was during junior high, and I had been invited for the first time to dinner with my boyfriend's family. I was madly in puppy love and wanted badly to make a good impression. I helped set the table, sat with my legs primly pressed together, put down my fork between bites, and smiled engagingly at my boyfriend's younger sister, seated next to me.

Then, just when everything was going very well, said younger sister let out a blast that practically levitated her off her seat. Then she sat back, looking exceedingly pleased with herself.

After a brief moment of shock, her father made a little play on words — we were having potatoes au gratin — about "cutting the cheese." The rest of the family smiled and acknowledged that, well, little girls will be little girls.

Meanwhile, where was I? Sliding off my chair as I shrieked and guffawed 'til my eyes filled with tears of embarrassment. Quite quickly, the attention and appall turned to me, clearly far more rude than the cheese cutter herself.

For years afterward, the mere word "cheese" could set off a flash-back. When I got word last year that the young lady in question had just had a child, the first thing I flashed on was that dinner table scene. To be quite honest, I am giggling right now as I stare at my computer screen.

I swear, it's pathetic.

I'm certainly not advocating a lack of appropriate etiquette. Like a burp or a sneeze, any emission should be discretely minimized and, when audible, briefly apologized for. But in order for that to happen, children need to be brought up knowing some things are just natural consequences.

You eat. You toot.

How to De-Gas Beans

What makes beans the musical fruit? It actually has to do with a sugar they contain that our bodies don't digest well and which tends to sit and ferment in the lower part of our digestive tract. But there are methods to reduce its effect. Personally, soaking is the only one of these I've tried, since it works pretty successfully, but many swear by the others. In our household, since flatulence produces hysterical laughter, we figure it can't be all bad.

#1: Soaking

This is the easiest method, though you'll need to be around the kitchen sporadically all day. Soak beans, completely covered with water, for 8-12 hours, draining and rinsing them about every three hours. Changing the water frequently is the key and very effective in eliminating the excess sugar starch — even if it is kind of a pain.

#2: Baking soda

Add a teaspoon of baking soda to 4 quarts of water. Stir in the dried beans and bring to a boil, then turn off heat and let beans soak at least four hours (or overnight). Drain, rinse and rinse again. The baking soda helps break down the bean's natural sugars without influencing the flavors of whatever recipe you use the beans for.

#3: Pressure cooking

If you have ever had a pressure cooker explode (as I have in the old days) you may be reluctant to test this method. But with today's Instant Pots, this is a quick and surefire method to breaking down the sugars.

Start by soaking the beans 4-8 hours, then draining and rinsing. Place beans in a pressure cooker with water to cover by about two inches. Set the pressure to high (or 15 pounds) and cook 10 to 12 minutes, followed by a slow pressure release. Drain, rinse again, and use in any recipe.

#4 SPICES/HERBS

Ajwain is an Indian spice (also known as carom seed) that tastes like a mix of cumin and thyme and is used for stomach upset in India (much as we use mint in America). Epazote is a herb native to Mexico and South America traditionally used in black bean dishes. Both are reportedly effective in reducing intestinal upset from cooked beans. Obviously, these spices do affect the flavor of the beans, so use them in appropriate recipes.

Scents and Sense-ability

THIS MORNING I POURED a cup of coffee, reflexively sniffed the milk carton, added a generous amount to my mug, and then watched in dismay as it curdled into unappetizing floating fragments. That's just one example of the disconcerting incidents I can attribute to having lost my sense of taste and smell after being diagnosed with Covid-19.

I was fortunate to be spared the worst of the threats after testing positive for the virus in Year One of the pandemic. I had fevers and chills, a headache and painful joints, but no cough, congestion, or breathing issues. Nausea kept me from eating anything but popsicles for a week, but even then, I know I could still smell because every aroma I inhaled just made me feel queasier.

It wasn't until I started to feel better — around week two — that I suddenly realized the chicken soup I was sipping was utterly tasteless. When I tried eating something more substantive, it felt like chewing on my own tongue. Texture and memory were all I had to decipher what I was eating, and they were sorely inadequate. In an effort to taste something — anything! — I found myself using inordinate amounts of salt, which did nothing to awaken my taste buds, but did manage to make every bite burn.

Given that I am alive and well today, you won't find me crying over spoiled milk. But while my taste buds have somewhat revived (albeit to a less-than-optimal degree), I'm still completely oblivious to the wafts of bacon, marijuana, or sewage that cause others to lick their lips or hold their noses.

It's a greater affliction than I ever imagined back in grade school, when my third-grade teacher asked — after a unit on Helen Keller — which of our five senses we'd be willing to part with. Back then, we all agreed losing the ability to smell would be preferable to going without sight, sound, touch, or taste.

But it turns out it's not quite that clear cut. Your sense of smell is inextricably wound up with your experience of taste. And frankly, because I can't smell, nothing tastes the way it used to. That leaves me feeling obstinately unfulfilled, like a child with Prader-Willi Syndrome in search of an eternally elusive satisfaction. The part of my brain that registers gustatory gratification seems permanently shut off.

People who've had to undergo a leg amputation sometimes have the phantom sensation that their limb is still there. I feel a little the same way about my nose, thinking I must be smelling the garlic and onions I'm cooking... only to realize I'm only remembering what it *should* smell like.

The loss of taste and smell is wearing, mentally and physically. It's depressing when mealtime, one of life's great pleasures, becomes more duty than delectation. While I'm not someone who needs to lose weight, if I didn't sometimes force down tasteless food now, I probably would have. (I've grown snippy with people who carry a few extra pounds saying they'd *love* to love food less. All I can say is, be careful what you wish for.)

As someone who's a free-wheeling experimenter in the kitchen, prone to taking liberties with recipes, cooking is more difficult too. I can no longer relish homemade bread baking in the oven, the pungent sting of wasabi, or the heady scent of herbs picked fresh from the garden. My recipe monitoring is totally off kilter. How much of any spice do you add when you can't rely on measuring "to taste"?

I even miss smells that are usually unpleasant: sulfuric water spraying from an irrigation system; hot asphalt laid by a road construction crew; an overloaded garbage truck on a summer day that leaves a pungent odor in its wake.

From the many articles I've read, this phenomenon lingers beyond a couple of weeks in only a tiny percentage of Covid survivors. (This reminds me of when I told my son, 20 years ago, that I'd been diagnosed with a benign brain tumor which occurs in only one of 100,000 people and he responded: "Wow! You're really special!") In desperation, I've tried every suggestion, from aromatherapy to acupuncture to essential oils. I've even practiced the mind exercises I'm told can "re-train" your olfactory nerves, but either I've got some belligerent nerves or a deficient mind.

When I was young, we used the drive to our cottage on Lake Michigan every summer, always along the same route. It wove through the town of Holland, Michigan, and past an industrial strip where there was a pickle factory and a bread bakery.

I have long forgotten the names of the streets, the look of the neighborhood, the pinching of the sister sitting next to me or the songs on the radio. But if I tip my head back, close my eyes and inhale deeply, I can instantly remember the intoxicating aroma as we passed the Bimbo bread factory and the briny, sour smell that permeated the car blocks before the Heinz plant came into view.

Oh what I wouldn't give to have that kind of sense-ability today.

Dill Pickles

During my biggest gardening/home canning years, I learned what worked best for making pickles (firm, small pickling cucumbers, fresh dill, and a grape leaf in each jar) and what didn't (older, bigger cucumbers and dried dill). If you have a garden and pick the cucumbers when they're no more than a pinky-length long, they're like French cornichons, crunchy and delicious. The sharp vinegary aroma in the kitchen when I'm making these brings me right back to those car rides to Lake Michigan.

Ingredients

- 6 pounds small pickling cucumbers

- 3 cups white vinegar

- 3 cups water

- 4 Tbsp. pickling salt *(don't use table salt or your pickles will end up limp)*

- 7 garlic cloves, peeled

- Dill weed and dill seed, fresh or dried

- 3 ½ tsp. whole black peppercorns

- Fresh or canned grape leaves

DIRECTIONS

1. Prepare canning jars by running them through the dishwasher and keeping them there to stay warm. Start bringing water in your canning pot to a boil.

2. Wash cucumbers and slice into spears if desired. (If they're small enough, I prefer leaving them whole.)

3. In a medium saucepan, over medium high heat, bring vinegar, water and salt to a boil.

4. In bottom of each jar place 1 garlic clove, at least 1 tsp. of dill seed and 1 tsp of dill weed and ½ tsp. of peppercorns. Pack cucumbers tightly into jar.

5. Fill jars to just below brim with the hot liquid mixture, making sure all cucumbers are covered but leaving ¼ inch of headspace at the top of the jar. Place a grape leaf (or half) on top.

6. Place lids on jars, screw on bands and wipe outside clean. Process I hot water bath approximately 10 minutes at a rolling boil. Remove jars, check seals and let cool. (If a jar doesn't seal, it can still be kept in the refrigerator.) Pickles are best if left to sit for at least a week.

Strawberries

WHEN I WALKED INTO the produce store the other day, I noticed there were flats of strawberries on sale.

It's that time of year when they are plump and plentiful and relatively cheap. They start you thinking about things like strawberry shortcake and strawberry jam and strawberry/rhubarb pudding with whipped cream and... Gramma Seidman.

Wait a minute. Where did that come from? She has been gone for more than 50 years now, my father's eccentric and not infrequently exasperating mother. And you'd be more likely to remember her for her valiant crusade to save the African Masai tribe or joining heart and cause with the hippies over the Vietnam War than for anything to do with strawberries.

After all, this was a woman who never got closer to a kitchen than to commend the chef for most of her 70-odd years. She dutifully took each of her 10 grandchildren out to "dunch" — her preferred midafternoon meal — at her favorite restaurant when they came home from college, but you knew better than to ask her to put on an apron and whip you up a little something to eat. To her, an apron was the wide part of the driveway where you parked the car.

This lack of domesticity was a distinct bonus when we were young and regularly spending Sunday afternoons at her big Tudor-style home overlooking a small lake in western Michigan, where an entire spacious "playroom" was devoted to holding every toy, book, and record a child could ever desire. (Ah, but that's another story.)

When you had a grandma who didn't know how to boil an egg and Sunday was the cook's day off, the meal was whatever came in the delivery truck from the specialty store and required no more preparation than twisting off a top or slicing through plastic.

Artichoke hearts. Greek olives. Shiny crackers in exotic shapes and colors from the Far East. Hearts of palm. Smoked oysters. Tiny cocktail franks to be skewered with toothpicks sporting frilly skirts. Kumquats. (Well, OK. Those weren't so enticing.) I was introduced to them all sitting at a table in the playroom's kid-size kitchen.

Some people lovingly remember their grandmother for her sweaty brow over a hot stove, her scent of cinnamon and brown sugar, or her light-as-air matzo balls. I remember mine for her fervent discussions about the ills of bralessness, the relish trays she brought to Thanksgiving dinners that were a point of pride because she'd lined up the purchased canned goods so attractively, and her devotion to a husband who lay dying in an upstairs bedroom for nearly a decade. I have an enormous collection of family recipes, but none of them came from her.

So why the strawberry connection? Well, in her waning years, long after her husband had died, her grandchildren had spread across the country, and the playroom goods had been donated to a local museum, Gramma Seidman developed a much postponed and entirely unexpected domestic interest.

I think of her now as "The Belated Cook."

At the ripe old age of 75, Gramma discovered the kitchen. She let the cook go, purchased a number of timesaving gadgets (the kind advertised on late night television), consulted a big, fat recipe book, and pretended that heating something up and creating a dish were one and the same. Now dunch took place at her home and was likely to consist of any number of strange concoctions broiled on top of an English muffin in a toaster oven.

And, in one final and grand hurrah, she created her magnum opus: a recipe for strawberry pie. This was a fairly mundane but well-received recipe she never failed to mention had a "secret ingredient."

As her sole epiphany of culinary creativity, she was loathe to reveal just what that secret was. (Though, because she would appreciate a brief moment of immortality in the kitchen, I will: a thin layer of softened cream cheese spread on the cooked crust just before the strawberry layer.) Nor did she admit the crust was store-bought and the whipped cream came from an aerosol can.

We played along and feigned ignorance, oohing and yumming over the novelty and politely neglecting to mention how much we missed the relish trays of exotic delicacies and the do-it-yourself dinners on a toothpick.

But now that she is gone, a flat of fat red berries at the store makes me miss The Belated Cook more than ever.

THE BELATED COOK'S STRAWBERRY PIE

Though Gramma Seidman did belatedly learn to cook a few things, she was far from a pastry chef. She bought frozen pie crusts, crimping the edges by hand to make them look homemade, and used aerosol whipped cream rather than making her own. I prefer my Mom's pie crust recipe (though mine never are as good as hers were) and freshly whipped cream. Your choice.

INGREDIENTS

- 1 *(9-inch)* pie crust, baked *(recipe below)*

- 1 quart fresh strawberries

- 1 cup white sugar

- 3 Tbsp. cornstarch

- ¾ cup water

- 4 oz. cream cheese, softened or whipped

- ½ cup heavy whipping cream

DIRECTIONS

1. Bake crust, cool. Gently spread softened cream cheese in an even layer on the crust. Arrange half the strawberries on top of cream cheese layer. Mash remaining berries and combine with sugar in medium saucepan. Place saucepan over medium heat, bring to a boil, stirring frequently.

2. In a small bowl, whisk together cornstarch and water. Gradually stir cornstarch mixture into boiling strawberry mixture. Reduce heat and simmer mixture until thickened, about 10 minutes, stirring constantly. Pour mixture over berries in pastry shell. Chill for several hours.

3. In a small bowl, whip cream until soft peaks form. Cover chilled strawberries with a layer of whipped cream. Place one perfect big strawberry in the center of the pie.

Mom's Pie Crust

Ingredients

- 2 cups flour

- ⅔ cup shortening *(Mom used Crisco, which is gross, but makes a great crust)*

- 1 teaspoon salt

- ¼ teaspoon baking powder

- 1/3 cup ice water *(to which Mom unhelpfully added, on my old recipe card "plus any more needed")*

Directions

1. Mix dry ingredients. Cut in shortening in three parts. Add water gradually, stirring gently to bind the dough. Do not knead.

2. Roll out dough to ¼" thickness on pastry cloth to a circumference an inch wider than the pie tin. Slide the crust into the tin, allowing it to overlap edges evenly. Double under the outside rim and crimp the edge using the inside of your thumb and your first finger.

3. Bake at 450 degrees for 10 minutes, then 350 until lightly browned.

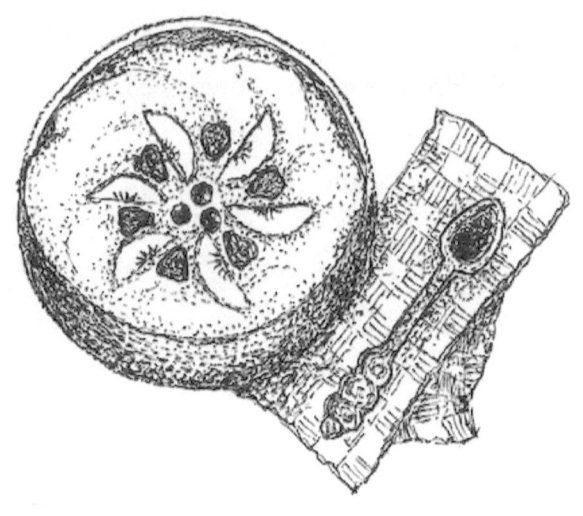

Food Consciousness

WE HAVE A LOVE/HATE relationship with food.

We love new tastes, exotic combinations, and unusual flavors that wake up our taste buds. We love the nostalgic, comfort dishes that make us remember childhood and home and family. We're excited to try new restaurants and to return to favorite haunts.

And yet, often, we hate food at the same time. We are bored by it, or obsessed with it, or weary of preparing it, or blame it for our increasing girth. Or we are just taking it for granted.

Three meals a day — or four or six depending on your habits — can become routine and mindless. Sometimes we stand in front of the open refrigerator, even after we have just gone grocery shopping — usually buying the same old things we always buy — and think: *There's nothing in here to eat.*

Living alone, as I have for most of my adult life, I've taken to wading through my backlog of New Yorkers as I consume my evening salad or soup or leftovers. I'm too tired, too uninspired, or just too hot to make much of anything else and I've never been a TV dinner kind of person, maybe because that was verboten in my childhood home. But, the other night, I was halfway through dinner before I realized I hadn't really tasted anything I was eating.

What am I doing? I thought. Am I eating because I have to or because I want to? Am I hungry? Satiated? Conscious? What's the point in eating if I'm not tasting?

I was reminded of my mother, a woman who for most of her life was a wonderful cook and an avid appreciator of fresh, healthy, taste-full food. She had a feel for how to balance a meal (in color, flavor, and nutrition) and an artist's eye for how to present it. Moreover, all of that was important to her, whether the dinner she was making was for Dad's high-profile Washington, D.C., friends or Sunday night soup and popcorn for her six children.

But 13 years before her death, she suffered a major stroke that left her partially paralyzed and with very little speech. It inexorably altered both her attitude toward, and her appetite for, food.

She couldn't make up her mind about what she wanted to eat anymore, or when or where she wanted to eat it. She couldn't cook or create a menu or cut her own meat. She couldn't even drive to the grocery store to select her own ingredients or longingly finger the glossy produce at a farmers market. What she did eat got stuck in the pocket of her cheek on the paralyzed side, to be dug out later with a finger as she brushed her teeth. Or, embarrassingly, leaked out of the corner of her mouth, leaving a snail's trail down to her chin.

On the rare occasions when she felt something like real hunger, she chose things so wildly divergent from her previous preferences — barbecue ribs, creamy-sauced pastas, or something deep-fried that inevitably left a greasy stain on her shirt — she seemed like another person than the one who'd opted for greens and salads and fruits her whole life.

Worst of all, at those infrequent times of appetite, she tended to eat too much too fast, unintentionally catalyzing in the rush of frenzied feeding a neurological response that resulted in her projectile vomiting whatever she'd consumed. It wasn't until years after her death, when I was reading a novel and the author named the not uncommon phenomenon after a character threw up a meal at the table, that I realized this is what my mother had suffered from.

Mealtimes became agonizingly tense and foreboding for us all as we waited for her body to reject what it had just consumed. How many times, with embarrassment and shame, did we call a waiter over to remove a plate, hastily covered with a cloth napkin? What greater curse than to see one of life's greatest pleasures turned into a constant and painful reminder of what she'd lost.

It didn't help that my father — who left the kitchen to his wife for most of their 65-year marriage — tried to take over as a well-meaning but inept chef when she could no longer navigate in the kitchen. His standards, if you could call them that, appalled my mother as much as his "middle dishing" had at family dinners. Bratwurst cut up on a paper plate with a dab of mustard may have satisfied his carnivorous bent, but it did not feed my mother's aesthetic sensibilities and was often dismissed with a wave of her one still functional hand without her having taken a single bite.

Several months before my parents' deaths (within six months of each other in 2009), I moved in to their Albuquerque condo to help with my mother's care during the evenings after her daytime aide went home. One morning when my father went into the kitchen to prepare her breakfast — stick a spoon in the yogurt container and put the basket of berries on the table — I shooed him out of the way and spent 10 minutes amusing myself by swirling the yogurt in a bowl and making an elaborate design of cut-up fruit on top before leaving for work.

I put it on the table, then went to get my mother. She sat down at her place, folded her hands in her lap, bowed her head — and burst into tears. It wasn't quite the reaction I'd hoped for. My father, uncomfortable as always with unfiltered emotions, pursed his lips and said, "She does that some mornings," and buried his head back in the Wall Street Journal.

But my mother, shaking her head from side to side, made clear she wasn't expressing disapproval, but just the opposite. She pointed at the design of fruit and, steeling herself to spit out the right word, said, "so... pret-ty." It was one of the few intelligible things she'd said since her aphasia began.

It took her the better part of an hour, but she ate every bite, with an artist's eye for preserving some design as she went along. Then she set down her spoon neatly, used her napkin and her good hand to wipe the dribble from her chin, and sat for a few more minutes looking distractedly into the distance, as if recalling memorable meals of the past.

I thought about that moment as I looked down at the dinner I'd assembled carelessly, eaten mindlessly, and tasted almost not at all. Then I put down my magazine and moved myself and my plate out to the back porch, where I ate the rest of my meal lingeringly, listening to grumbles of thunder, smelling a new rain and cultivating an awareness of every bite.

Acknowledgements

No book is written without a host of helpers. Among the many people who have supported me and my work, I am especially grateful to:

The late Barbara Page, former *Albuquerque Tribune* copy editor extraordinaire and the first and fiercest fan of the "Place at the Table" column;

Arthur Pincus, my former editor at the *New York Times* and career-long writing mentor and coach;

My son, Keaton, who changed my life in every way for the better and who continues to think everything I cook for him tastes great.

And most of all, my parents, who exposed me to great food, bountiful gardens, and good manners, and my beloved siblings — Tom, Tracy, Sarah, Meg, and Robin — who were my first tablemates and remain my favorite dinner companions.

About the Author & Illustrator

CARRIE SEIDMAN is an award-winning career newspaper journalist who has served on the staffs of the *New York Times*, the *Los Angeles Herald-Examiner*, the *Albuquerque Journal*, and *Albuquerque Tribune*. Since 2010 she has served as a columnist, dance critic, and arts writer for the *Sarasota Herald-Tribune* on Florida's Gulf coast.

Seidman's columns, reviews, and long-form narratives have earned honors from local, state, and national journalism and mental health organizations, including Mental Health America's National Media Award and the Florida Society of Newspaper Editor's Gold Medal for Public Service. Her previous book, *FACEing Mental Illness: The Art of Acceptance*, showcased profiles and artwork from her award-winning year-long mental health fellowship project for the Carter Center for Mental Health Journalism.

A graduate of Barnard College and the Columbia University School of Journalism, Seidman is the mother of a one adult son who lives with genetic and mental health disorders. A two-time breast cancer survivor and lifelong dancer, she enjoys ballroom dancing, yoga, and long-distance walking.

Author photo by Cliff Roles

TRACY SEIDMAN (1951-2023) was an award-winning artist and illustrator, as well as the longtime manager of a working cattle ranch for 50 years. She is renowned for her pine needle baskets, embellished with beadwork, flint, and porcupine quills, created in the authentic Native American tradition, as well as for uniquely creative maps of Southwestern ranches.

The divorced parent of two adult children, she spent most of her life on the Wagon Mound Ranch in remote northeastern New Mexico, outside the small village of Wagon Mound. It is there she was buried after succumbing to an inoperable brain cancer in August 2023, just before this book was completed. These illustrations are among the last works of art she created.

Stories Take Flight at Ibis Books

The IBIS is sacred to Thoth,
the Egyptian god of learning,
inventor of writing,
and scribe to the gods.

They are gregarious birds that live,
travel, and breed in flocks.

And they are legendary for their courage.

ibis-books.com